12.90

SCIENCE/
TECHNOLOGY/
SOCIETY
PROJECTS FOR
YOUNG SCIENTISTS

DAVID E. NEWTON

SCIENCE/ TECHNOLOGY/ SOCIETY PROJECTS FOR YOUNG SCIENTISTS

PROJECTS FOR YOUNG SCIENTISTS
FRANKLIN WATTS 1991
NEW YORK / LONDON / TORONTO / SYDNEY

Photographs copyright © : Roger A. Smith: pp. 14, 18, 19; Photo Researchers, Inc.: pp. 40 (Joe Munroe), 51 (Russ Kinne), 54 (David Plowden), 56, 68 (both Lynn McLaren), 72 (Ray Ellis), 75 (Kit & Max Hunn), 77 (Christa Armstrong), 89 (Herman Emmet), 92 top, 95 (both Tom McHugh), 106 (Gordon S. Smith); Gamma-Liaison: pp. 59 (S. Anger), 98 (Bob Riha); Southern California Edison: p. 92 bottom.

Library of Congress Cataloging-in-Publication Data

Newton, David E.
Science/technology/society projects for young scientists / David
E. Newton.
p.   cm. — (Projects for young scientists)
Includes bibliographical references and index.
Summary: Offers guidelines for a variety of experiments and
projects related to science, technology, and society.
ISBN 0-531-11047-8
1. Science—Experiments—Juvenile literature. 2. Engineering—
Experiments—Juvenile literature. 3. Science—Social aspects—
Juvenile literature 4. Engineering—Social aspects—Juvenile
literature. [1. Science—Experiments. 2. Engineering—
Experiments. 3. Science—Social aspects. 4. Engineering—Social
aspects. 5. Experiments.] I. Title. II. Series.
Q164.N48   1991   91-17825 CIP AC
507.8—DC20

CONTENTS

To Kathy Nichols,
with great appreciation to a good friend,
a true buddy, through thick and thin

1

SCIENCE, TECHNOLOGY, AND SOCIETY

A lot of people in your community don't know about Duncan's Hollow. But you do. You and your friends have played there for years. You've come to know the hollow as well as your own backyard. That's the reason you know about the Duncan's Hollow butterfly and the threat to its survival.

Magnum Developers wants to build a housing development in the hollow. You know how badly the community needs new housing. But building in the hollow is likely to destroy the milkweed plants on which the Duncan's Hollow butterfly feeds. Biologists at the local college say the butterfly will not survive this intrusion on its territory. Since the hollow is the only place in the world the species is known to live, development may doom it to extinction.

Is new housing in Duncan's Hollow really worth the loss of the Duncan's Hollow butterfly?

The Duncan's Hollow issue is fictitious. But it is typical of the kinds of questions humans face in every part of the world today. For example:

1. How can we dispose of all the plastic we use without damaging the environment?

2. Should we cut back on the use of private automobiles if that will help reduce air pollution?

3. Is it worth using certain pesticides to grow "perfect" fruit even if we aren't sure about the health effects of those pesticides?

4. Should we build more nuclear power plants to generate electricity, given what we know about the safety of those plants?

Issues such as these all have one thing in common. They involve problems in science and technology that are closely related to the rest of our lives. Thus, they are often called science/technology/society, or STS, issues.

STS issues are difficult because they can be solved only when all aspects of the problem—scientific, technological, economic, political, sociological, and ethical—are understood and considered. In many cases, experts from all these fields may be involved in the solution of a particular STS issue.

STS PROJECTS

This book describes a number of STS projects in which you may be interested. These projects take many different forms. Some are scientific experiments. An experiment is a project in which you study one part of the natural world under controlled conditions.

For example, you might want to find out what factors affect the way a pea plant grows. One way to answer that question would be to study pea plants growing in the field. You could start by fencing off a piece of land where pea plants are growing. Then you would find ways to control factors that affect plant growth, such as amount of water, light, and fertilizer. You could also do the experiment indoors, perhaps in a greenhouse. That way you could control growing factors more easily.

Scientists have developed very clear rules about conducting an experiment. One rule is that you should never test more than one factor at a time. Suppose you changed both the amount of water and the amount of fertilizer used on your test patch of peas. When you observed how the peas grew, you could not tell which factor—light or fertilizer—made the peas grow that way.

Another rule is to measure everything you can. It is much more informative to say that a pea plant grew 5 cm in one week than it is to say the plant grew "a lot" since the last time you looked. A science teacher or adult friend can tell you more about the correct way to design and carry out a scientific experiment. Or you can refer to some of the books listed in the bibliography at the end of this book.

Other STS projects are surveys. In one type of survey, you ask people what they think about a particular issue. For example, you might want to find out how the people in your community feel about building a nuclear power plant nearby. At first, surveys seem like easy projects to do. You just go out into the neighborhood and ask people, "How do you feel about building a nuclear power plant at the edge of town?"

But surveys are actually quite difficult to do well. Some typical problems of surveys are asking unfair questions or interviewing only certain kinds of people. For example, you might ask people why they think nuclear power plants are so terrible. But this is an unfair question since it starts out by assuming that a nuclear power plant is bad. You might decide to interview only the people who live in your neighborhood. But are your neighbors typical of other people in the community? If they are not, the answers will have limited value. They only tell you how part of the community feels about the issue.

As with scientific experiments, surveys should always be carefully planned according to strict rules. Make sure your questions are fair and that you survey a representative group of people. A teacher or adult friend may be able to tell you more about designing a good survey.

Other STS projects involve mathematical analysis. One way to learn about population problems, for example, is to make a graph of past population changes. The graph gives you a clear, simple way of seeing what has happened in the past and predicting what might happen in the future. You may want to consult your math teacher about STS projects that require mathematical analysis.

STS projects usually involve science. But an STS project is different from other science projects you may have done in biology, chemistry, physics, or other science classes. The difference is that STS projects include nonscience factors as well. Studying the growth of peas is a science project. But finding out how to increase the yield of peas in order to feed undernourished people is an STS project. You would have to think about the cost of growing peas, the laws that may be needed to give peas away, the customs that may have to be changed to get people to grow peas rather than some other crop, the educational programs that farmers and consumers may require, the advertising campaigns that might be necessary to change people's attitudes, and so on.

YOUR PROJECT
GOALS

What can you hope to accomplish by doing the STS projects in this book? Most of these projects deal with large, complex, community, state, national, and international issues. The projects you do will probably not solve any of these issues. However, the work you do on the projects can be very helpful. For one thing, the projects will help you better understand the issues. They will also teach you some skills that can be used in attacking STS problems. They may draw the attention of other people in the community to these issues and point out some ways of attacking them. With luck, your projects may actually move some problems closer to a resolution.

The projects in the book usually focus on "your community." The term *community* refers to the geographic area in which you live and the people who live there. It could mean a small town, a middle-sized city, a rural area, or a neighborhood in a large city. You decide what "community" means to you. Then use that definition of the term in these projects.

The projects focus on issues in the local community because this is the easiest level for you to work on. You can actually do pollution tests on a local pond, interview the local director of public health, study land erosion on nearby farms, and do other firsthand projects.

But most STS issues extend far beyond a single community. Your town may be able to resolve the Duncan's Hollow controversy. But it can deal with only one small part of the state's waste disposal problems, the nation's acid rain problems, or the world's ozone problems.

Unfortunately, working on a state, national, or international level can be difficult. You may end up reading about an issue rather than working on it firsthand. But broader views of STS issues—at state, national, and international levels—are very important. Wherever possible in these projects, you should look for ways to expand your research to other levels. Many communities, for example, have chapters of Greenpeace, the Sierra Club, Planned Parenthood, and other organizations concerned with STS issues. Go to these organizations for information, advice, and opportunities to work on issues that concern and interest you. The appendix provides a list of organizations concerned with STS issues.

This project on air pollution may be "close to home"
—an ideal STS "community" and science fair project.

ADULT PARTNERS

In many projects, you are asked to find an adult partner who will work with you. The adult partner should be someone who can give you information, tell you where to look for information, accompany you to locations in the community you want to visit, help you design and interpret questionnaires, and assist you in other ways. Some people you might ask to be an adult partner are a parent, an adult relative, an adult neighbor, a government official, a local high school or college teacher, or a worker at a local company.

One situation in which you must have an adult partner who is a qualified science teacher is any project that involves the use of chemicals. The book provides specific warnings about any chemicals you may have to use. These warnings should never excuse you from finding a science teacher or another expert to help you with the project.

You should also call on your adult partner during the planning phase of projects. Some of the projects in this book are described in detail. You will know exactly what steps to carry out. But many projects are only outlined, and some are simply suggested. In these instances, you will have to design the project yourself. You will always want to have an adult partner help you with plans. The adult partner may mention ideas you have not thought about and will warn you about potentially dangerous procedures.

SOME SAFETY SUGGESTIONS

Safety is always an important consideration when doing any STS project. As you plan your research, always try to think of any risks or dangers that may arise in your research. Always talk with your adult partner about these dangers and make sure you know how to avoid them.

To help you plan for safe projects, the book contains special safety notes for those projects in which knowing about risks is especially important. Read these notes very carefully, make sure you understand them, discuss them with your adult partner, and then follow them closely.

You should also get in the habit of remembering some general safety rules when doing any kind of experiment or field research. The following list includes some of those rules. Talk with your adult partner about these rules and about any other rules she or he may recommend to you.

1.   Always wear safety goggles when working with any kind of chemical or with flames.

2.   Always wear a lab apron, lab coat, or some other kind of protective clothing when working in a lab or with hazardous materials anywhere.

3.   Always assume that any chemical is toxic (poisonous) and harmful to your eyes, nose, skin, and clothing. Many chemicals are not dangerous. But you will be safer if you treat all chemicals with respect. Wash thoroughly with water if you spill any chemicals on yourself and when you are through working with chemicals.

4.   Be very cautious with open flames.

5.   Always know where safety equipment is located and how to use it. The safety equipment you should know about includes a fire extinguisher, an eyewash, a safety shower, and a fire blanket.

6.   Always conduct projects under supervision of your adult partner. Always do field studies or experiments with an adult partner present.

HOW TO USE STS PROJECTS

You may have chosen to read this book for any number of reasons. You may simply want to know more about the ways that science, technology, and society interact in our society. Or you may be interested in some specific issue in the community, such as its waste disposal problems. Or you may be looking for a project for your science class or a science fair.

All of the projects in this book can be used for science fairs. Some of the projects are scientific experiments on which you can expand. For example, you should be able to think of many variations on the plant-growing projects in chapter 3.

Other projects can be modified to have a stronger scientific component. For example, the mathematical study of population is called demography. Projects in chapter 8 can be changed and adapted to include more demographic studies. Also, most science fair judges today recognize that the social aspects of science and technology are very important and are legitimate science fair topics. This means you can pick specific questions presented throughout this book, expand on them, and turn them into interesting and worthwhile science fair projects.

These projects can also be used as classroom activities, not only in science, but also in health, history, civics, government, family living, and other social studies classes. Perhaps you belong to a school, church, or service club that is interested in local STS issues. The projects in this book may also be interesting activities for such organizations.

Before using a project for a class or a club, talk with your teacher or adviser to find out what kind of emphasis he or she would recommend for your project.

PROJECT REPORTS

Whatever your reason for starting a project, every project should end with a report. Your project report should describe what you did in the project, what information you collected, and how you interpret these findings.

The term "report" may mean to you a written report, such as the reports you may have written for laboratory

STS projects, such as "Marine Debris and Our
Environment," fit in fine at a science fair.

Both student (left) and professional science reports present the results of scientific investigations.

work in a science class. Such reports are perfectly acceptable. Government agencies, private interest groups, and companies spend huge amounts of time writing reports on all kinds of STS issues. In fact, those reports will be a valuable resource for you in many of the projects described in this book.

But think creatively about the reports you write. One of the problems with many reports is that they are not very interesting. They may contain valuable information and important recommendations. But people find it difficult to wade through page after page of boring text.

Consider other types of reports. For example, you might produce a slide show that illustrates what you did and what you learned in your project. Other means of reporting include films and videotapes, audiotapes, posters, bulletin board displays, models, illustrated lectures, and advertising campaigns. Even if you do end up writing a report, try to make it more interesting for your readers by using pictures, graphs, charts, and other devices that catch the attention.

Finally, keep in mind the individuals and groups who will be interested in the results of your project. One nice thing about STS projects is that they always involve real-life issues that interest people. Whatever you find out about air pollution, food additives, or population growth will interest someone in your community, in the state, or in the nation. Find out who that "someone" is and be sure that he, she, or they get copies of your report.

A NOTE ABOUT UNITS OF MEASUREMENT

Metric units are used exclusively in scientific research. British units are most commonly used in everyday life in the United States. In this book, we use metric units in most situations, such as measuring lengths, finding volumes, and determining weights. British units are used where they are the common form of measurement as, for example, in the description of a "10-gallon" aquarium tank or "a cup" of dirt.

2

FOOD AND NUTRITION

Nutrition is a subject about which everyone should know. Eating the right foods and the right amounts of each food is necessary for proper growth and good health. Scientists know a lot about the kind of diet best for teenagers, babies, young children, older men and women, pregnant women, and those who are ill.

Eating properly today has been made easier by the food industry. Most Americans can choose from a wide variety of attractive, tasteful, and healthful foods all year round. Yet, in spite of the knowledge we have of good nutrition and the availability of foods, many people do not eat as well as they should.

Many factors contribute to poor nutritional habits. Some people are so busy that they don't think about good eating habits. They grab a soda, a candy bar, or a bag of potato chips for lunch or dinner. Or meals may be gobbled in a few minutes at a fast-food restaurant.

Also, much of the food we eat today is highly processed. Vitamins and other nutrients are often lost during processing. Chemicals are commonly added to extend the shelf life of packaged foods. Additives are also used to change the color, taste, aroma, appearance, or other properties of a food. The very technology that provides such a wide range of foods also makes good nutrition more difficult.

EVALUATING YOUR OWN DIET

How healthful are your own eating habits? To answer that question, you need two sets of information. First, you need to know what kinds and amounts of foods nutrition experts think young people should have each day. Table 1 provides this information.

Second, you need to know the nutritional value of various foods. The best single source for this information is the U.S. Department of Agriculture's booklet "Nutritive Values of Foods." Ask your school librarian or dietitian for this or a similar reference.

Also, food labels provide nutritional information for many foods. Finally, many fast-food restaurants now publish nutritional information on the items they sell.

For this project, keep a careful record of all the food you eat each day for one week. Calculate the number of Calories and the amounts of protein, fat, vitamins, and minerals for each item you eat. How does your diet for the week compare with the recommendations in Table 1?

FAST FOODS AND PACKAGED FOODS

A hundred years ago, most of the foods people ate came from local sources: a home garden or a nearby dairy, for example. Today your diet is probably very different. It probably includes a large number of foods from two sources your grandparents had never heard of: fast foods and processed foods.

TABLE 1. RECOMMENDED DAILY ALLOWANCES FOR CERTAIN NUTRIENTS FOR TEENAGE BOYS AND GIRLS

	Boys	Girls
Energy	2800 Calories (2100–3900)	2100 Calories (1200–3000)
Fats	No more than 35% of total energy intake	
Protein	56 g	45 g
Vitamin A	1000 μg	800 μg
Thiamine	1.4 mg	1.1 mg
Riboflavin	1.6 mg	1.6 m
Niacin	18 mg	14 mg
Vitamin C	60 mg	60 mg
Vitamin D	10 μg	10 μg
Sodium	900–2700 mg	900–2700 mg
Calcium	1200 mg	1200 mg
Iron	10 mg	10 mg

What portion of your week's nutrients came from these two sources? In what ways did each source improve your diet? In what ways did they provide inadequate nutrition?

Look back at your own diet analysis for the week. For which nutrients was your consumption too high? For which was it too low? In what ways did fast-food items contribute to good nutrition? In what ways did they contribute to poor nutrition? Prepare a report that shows the advantages and disadvantages of a diet that includes a large fraction of fast-food items. Make a poster that presents your findings to other teenagers in an attractive and interesting way.

Repeat your diet analysis for packaged foods. Are some packaged foods in your diet more healthful than others? Are some less healthful? For example, are canned fruits more or less likely to be healthful than frozen fruits or fresh fruits? Are cookies made from frozen batter more or less nutritious than cookies that come in a box? Is the nutritional value of dried soups any different from that of canned soups?

Write and illustrate a "public service" pamphlet on the nutritional value of processed foods. Select any one kind of food (vegetables, fruits, soups, cakes, etc.) to focus on. Compare the nutritional values of the food in its various possible forms (fresh, frozen, canned, dried, etc.).

FOOD ADDITIVES

Take a look at a variety of food labels. One part of the label tells how much of each nutrient is present in the food. The second part of the label lists all items contained in the food. These ingredients are listed in descending order from the ingredient present in the largest amount to the one present in the smallest amount. Some of these ingredients—food additives—may have no nutritional value. They are added to the food for other reasons, for example, to keep the food from spoiling, to add flavor or color, or to keep the food from "caking." You can design and carry out a number of projects to learn more about food additives.

The very first food additives were those used to prevent spoilage. People who lived in cold regions had to find a way, for example, to keep food from spoiling during the winter when they had no fresh foods. Salting, curing, drying, and freezing are some of these methods. In this project you will test the effectiveness of various methods of food preservation.

After you put on your safety goggles, begin by steriliz-
ing about a dozen baby-food jars and their lids. You can
sterilize them by heating them in boiling water for about
five minutes.

Next, prepare a batch of oatmeal. Use dry oatmeal
that has nothing added to it. Make two cups of hot oatmeal according to directions on the package. Wearing
cloth gloves and using tongs, remove the jars from the
boiling water.

Place one teaspoon of prepared oatmeal into each
of the sterilized baby-food jars. **Caution:** Use cloth gloves
to handle the jars. Don't burn yourself on the hot jar!

To each of four jars, add one of the items listed below. Screw the top on the jar immediately after adding
the item.

Jar 1: A pinch of salt
Jar 2: A pinch of sugar
Jar 3: A pinch of borax
Jar 4: A pinch of baking soda

Screw the tops on jars 5 and 6. Place jar 5 in a freezer
and jar 6 in a refrigerator.

Heat jar 7 in boiling water for 30 seconds. You can
use the same pan of boiling water used to sterilize the jars
originally, or ask your adult partner to set up a water bath
for you to use. At the end of 30 seconds, immediately screw
the top on the jar.

Think of other methods of food preservation for the
remaining jars of oatmeal.

Finally, use one jar of oatmeal as a control, for comparison with other jars. Screw the top on the jar and set it
where it will not be disturbed.

Each day, examine each jar of oatmeal. Look for visible signs of spoilage. If you see evidence that the oatmeal has begun to spoil, open the jar and smell its con-
tents. Make a note of all indications that the oatmeal has

spoiled. **Caution:** Do not taste the oatmeal! Even if there are no visible signs or odors indicating spoilage, the oatmeal may contain dangerous microorganisms. When you have finished your project, dispose of all oatmeal samples in a safe way, as directed by your adult partner.

• Which method of food preservation worked best? Which worked least well? Make a list of the methods you tried, arranging them in order from most to least effective.

• Are there ways you can make some methods of preservation more effective? For example, would two pinches of salt be twice as effective a food preservative as one pinch? Would three, four, or ten pinches be three, four, or ten times as effective? Would a pinch of salt and a pinch of sugar be more effective than one pinch of either? Would oatmeal stored at −15° C last longer than oatmeal stored at 0° C? Devise a method for testing any of these ideas that interests you.

• Food processing companies today can select from a rather wide variety of chemicals to use as food preservatives. Among these are benzoic acid; sodium benzoate; calcium and sodium propionate; calcium, potassium, and sodium sorbate; and sodium and potassium sulfite. Ask a chemistry teacher for a small sample (no more than a half-teaspoon) of one or more of these chemicals. Add each chemical you receive to a jar of oatmeal, as you did in the original experiment above. Compare the effectiveness of each chemical you try with the preservation methods used in the original experiment. How does doubling or tripling the amount of a chemical affect its effectiveness as a preservative?

• A method that works well in preserving oatmeal might not work well with other foods. For example, suppose you wanted to keep a potato, a jar of milk, a piece of meat, an apple, or a loaf of home-baked bread from spoiling. Which of the above methods of preservation would work best with each of those foods? Invent a project that will allow you to answer this question.

RISKS AND BENEFITS
OF FOOD ADDITIVES

The food industry uses hundreds of different chemicals in foods today. Each chemical changes food in some helpful way. But questions have been raised about some food additives. Are we sure these chemicals are safe enough to use in our foods? The purpose of the next project is to help you learn more about chemicals added to our foods, the reasons they are added, and possible risks they may pose to human health.

First, collect a list of chemicals used as food additives. Begin by reading the labels on cans, jars, bottles, and other food containers in your home. Then visit local grocery stores to examine other food labels. Try to get the names of at least twenty-five food additives.

Make a chart like the one in Table 2 for these chemicals. The first column in the chart contains the name of the food additive. The second explains how and why the chemical is used. In this example, gum acacia is used to thicken a product. The third column lists objections raised to the use of this food additive. This example indicates that some critics claim that studies have never been made of possible health risks from the use of gum acacia.

TABLE 2. BENEFITS AND RISKS OF FOOD ADDITIVES (SAMPLE)

Food Additive	Uses	Possible Health Risks
Cyclamates	Sweetening agent	Causes cancer in test animals such as rats
Gum acacia	Thickening agent	No tests done on safety
Malic acid	Flavoring agent	Safe for adults; not tested on infants

You can get the information needed for columns 2 and 3 of the chart from various sources. Start with chemistry textbooks, chemical reference books, recent magazine articles on food additives, and the bibliography at the end of this book. Also, consult with your science teacher or librarian or a representative from the local health department.

• Some food additives are perfectly safe. No one worries about the prudent use of casein, for example, as a food additive. Casein occurs naturally in cow's milk. But other chemicals are the source of some concern. Which food additives that you studied fall into the latter category? Does the value of these chemicals as food additives outweigh any potential risk they may pose to human health? Prepare a report on one food additive whose use might be questionable. Point out the pros and cons of using this additive. Then make your own recommendation about its continued use in foods.

• Some people criticize certain food products because they contain large amounts of "synthetic foods." At one time, for example, you could have purchased a lemon pie that contained no natural foods at all. The pie was *all* synthetic chemicals and food additives. Can you find a food product similar to this one, a product that consists entirely or mostly of synthetic chemicals and food additives? If so, should there be any objection to selling this product or other products like it?

Choose any one highly synthetic food on which to prepare a report. Explain why you think this food product is or is not a worthwhile consumer product.

TESTING FOR FOOD ADDITIVES

Safety Notes
1. Wear safety goggles, gloves, and a lab coat or apron while doing this project.

2. Dilute sulfuric acid is toxic and can burn your skin and clothing. Use it with care. If you spill any on yourself, wash it off with water.

3. Iodine solutions are poisonous. If you get iodine on your hands, wash it off well with water.

Notes about Materials
1. You can make a starch solution by making a paste of 1 g of soluble starch with 5 mL of cold water. Then dilute the paste with 100 mL of boiling water.

2. Ask your science teacher for about 50 mL of a 0.01 N iodine solution to use in this project.

Analyzing food for the presence of additives is often difficult. In many cases, only small amounts of the additive are used, and sophisticated equipment is needed to detect it. In some cases, however, a food additive can be relatively easy to detect. The test for sulfur dioxide is one you can do. **Be sure to ask your science teacher to help you with these projects.**

Sulfur dioxide is used to preserve certain foods, most commonly, dried fruits. You can test for sulfur dioxide in foods with a starch–iodine test. To see how that test works, place 100 mL of distilled water in a flask. Add 1 to 2 mL of dilute (6N) sulfuric acid and 2 mL of a starch suspension. Then, with a medicine dropper, add iodine solution one drop at a time until the solution in the flask turns blue and retains its color for 1 minute. Count the number of drops needed to produce a lasting blue color.

This experiment shows how the starch–iodine test works on a "blank," a sample that contains no sulfur dioxide. Keep a record of the number of drops of iodine solution needed to change the color of this blank solution.

Now choose a food to test for sulfur dioxide. For example, combine about 50 g of dried fruit with an equal amount of water in a food blender. Blend the mixture thoroughly, then strain the liquid through cheesecloth until you get a clear solution. A clear solution is one that contains no solid pieces of fruit in it. Test the solution with the starch–iodine test as you did above.

The iodine you add drop by drop will first react with sulfur dioxide in the fruit. When the sulfur dioxide is all used up, the iodine will cause the starch to turn blue, as it did in the blank. By counting the number of drops of iodine solution added to the fruit mixture, you have a measure of the amount of sulfur dioxide added to the dried fruit. Remember to subtract the number of drops of iodine solution needed for the blank.

• Repeat the test with other foods that you know or suspect to contain sulfur dioxide. Compare the amount of sulfur dioxide present in various foods.

• The same test can be used to detect the presence of sulfites in foods. Design a project that will compare the amount of sulfite added to various foods.

• What objections, if any, are there to the use of sulfur dioxide and sulfites in foods? Are acceptable substitutes available for these food additives? Prepare a report on the use of sulfur dioxide and sulfites as food additives. Point out the advantages and disadvantages of using these two food additives.

CHANGING AMERICAN DIETS

During the 1940s, Americans consumed an average of more than 400 pounds of milk per person each year. By the 1980s, that number had dropped to less than 250 pounds per person per year. In 1910, Americans ate mostly fresh fruit and almost no processed (canned, dried, frozen, etc.) fruit, 125 pounds of fresh compared with less than 5 pounds of processed fruit. By the 1980s, Americans were eating nearly equal amounts of fresh and processed fruits.

These two examples show how different the eating habits of Americans today are from those of earlier generations. In what other areas do you think eating patterns have changed? Construct a series of graphs that show how the amounts of various foods consumed by Americans have changed in the last 50 to 100 years.

You can get the information you need from the *Statistical Abstract of the United States,* published by the Bureau of the Census, from almanacs, and from other references. Ask your librarian for help in locating the references you need.

Do an analysis of one or more of the graphs you have made. Why has consumption of the food(s) you have chosen to study increased or decreased? What has been the effect on people's nutrition because of that increase or decrease? What recommendations do you have for future production and consumption of these foods?

NUTRITION KNOWLEDGE

People will eat healthful foods provided that (1) they know what constitutes good nutritional practice and (2) they are willing to base their own eating habits on that knowledge. For this project, try to learn more about the nutrition knowledge your friends and neighbors possess.

Begin by writing a questionnaire that tests a person's knowledge of good nutritional practices. Some sample questions include the following:

1. How many Calories do experts believe that you (the person being interviewed) should have in one day?

2. Name any one vitamin and tell why it is important for good health.

3. List three foods that are a good source of iron.

4. When should a person consider taking vitamin pills?

Here are some suggestions for writing and using the questionnaire:

1. Do not make the questionnaire too long. About ten questions will be enough.

2. Make the questions simple and easy to understand. A person should be able to answer each question in a few words.

3. Try to interview a variety of individuals, males and females, young and old.

Work with your adult partner in writing the questionnaire and interpreting the responses you get from your interviews.

What do the results of your project tell you about nutrition knowledge among your friends and neighbors? Is it excellent? Good? Fair? Poor? Where did the people you spoke with get their knowledge about nutrition? Outline an educational program that would improve the nutrition knowledge among this group of individuals.

3

AGRICULTURE

The most important task facing any society is to find ways to feed its people. Until quite recently, most families raised their own food. They grew the crops, raised the animals, and caught the fish they needed for themselves. They bought or traded only a small fraction of the food they needed.

Today, that situation has changed dramatically. In many nations, the United States included, only a small fraction of the population actually produces food. Most people never see the means of production: farms, dairies, ranches, and fishing fleets. They buy and consume foods produced days, weeks, or months earlier at locations hundreds or thousands of miles away.

These changes have been made possible by a number of scientific and technological developments, including hybrid seeds, chemical pesticides and fertilizers, and modern machinery. In this chapter you will find projects from which you can learn more about the methods of modern agriculture and about the problems they sometimes pose for society.

CHANGING PATTERNS OF AMERICAN AGRICULTURE

The American farm looks very different in the 1990s from the way it did in the 1890s. The changed character of the farm has had both beneficial and harmful effects on modern American society.

You can learn more about the evolution of American agriculture by studying various characteristics of the agricultural system. One helpful way to study these characteristics is by making graphs that show how agriculture has changed over the past three centuries. Find the information you need to make a graph for each of the following characteristics:

1. The average size of an American farm.

2. The percentage of the American population engaged in agriculture.

3. The average yield of food (in Calories per acre or some other measure).

4. The average amount of energy spent to raise one kilogram of food or spent on one acre of farmland.

5. The number of fish caught in U.S. waters or by U.S. fishing fleets.

6. The fraction of an American's annual income spent on food.

7. Farm productivity (measured by the number of hours of labor needed to produce one pound of food).

Examine the graphs you have made. Think of factors that may explain any trends you see. For example, the greater use of machinery may explain the decrease in the number of people working in agriculture (see 2 above).

Next, outline some benefits that have resulted from

the changes you discover. For example, in 6 above you may find that Americans now spend less on food than they once did. That allows them to spend more money on other items.

Finally, look for any problems resulting from the trends you uncover. For example, changes in farm size (1) may create problems for people who want to work in agriculture (problems such as . . .).

STUDYING AGRICULTURAL METHODS WITH A MODEL PLOT

You can devise many projects to study the agricultural methods used today. One way to do these projects is to construct a model plot like the one shown on page 36. This model plot consists of a large wooden box filled with dirt. The box is lined with heavy plastic to make it waterproof. The box also contains a few holes along the sides, at the bottom, to allow water to drain out. The tray below the box catches water that drains through the dirt in the box. As you do projects with the model plot, you will probably find ways to make it more useful for your research.

Remember to place your model plot where it can get enough sunlight to keep alive the plants growing in it.

EFFECTS OF SOIL TYPES

Growing plants need various nutrients. Nitrogen, phosphorus, and potassium are the most important of these nutrients. Plants often get the chemicals they need from the soil in which they are growing. Soils are richer or poorer in various nutrients. Thus, the nature of soil partly determines how well plants grow.

Soil is a mixture of four components: clay, silt, sand, and humus. The first three are distinguished by the size of particles. Clay is made of very small particles, silt of slightly larger particles, and sand of still larger particles. Humus is material produced by the decay of leaves, grass, and other organic matter.

Divide your model plot into twelve sections. You can use pieces of stiff plastic to separate the sections from each other. Fill the twelve sections as follows:

1. Pure sand.

2. Pure silt.

3. Pure clay.

4. Pure humus.

5. Sand and clay.

6. Sand and humus.

7. Clay and humus.

8. Silt and humus.

9. All four components.

10–12. Soil samples from three different locations in your neighborhood.

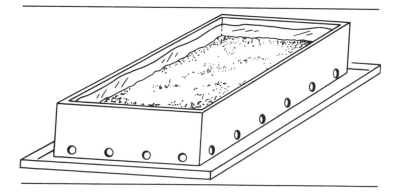

**Building a model plot is a good way
to study agricultural techniques.**

For samples 10 to 12, collect about four cups of soil from your backyard, from the school yard, from an open field, from nearby woods, or from any other location. Try to collect clean, natural soil that does not contain broken glass, plastic, waste paper, metal, or other waste materials from human activities.

Plant six radish seeds in each section. Water the sections evenly until the seeds sprout and the plants have each grown four leaves. Find a way to keep careful records of the rate at which plants grow in each section. For example, you might record the number of days it takes for seeds to sprout in each section. Then, each day, you could measure the height of the growing plants. Graph the rate at which plants grow in each type of soil.

You can repeat this project using different combinations of sand, silt, clay, and humus. Can you find a soil composition that will be best for growing plants? Do other kinds of plants grow best in the same soil? Or do beans, corn, wheat, and other plants require different kinds of soil? Devise projects that will answer these questions for you.

EFFECTS OF FERTILIZERS

Soils may not contain all the nutrients plants need to grow properly. Most farmers today add nutrients in the form of fertilizers to their soils. Some fertilizers are natural. For example, waste products from animals—manure—is a good natural fertilizer. Other fertilizers are synthetic, or "chemical." Chemical fertilizers are specially designed and produced to deliver certain combinations of nutrients.

The label on every bag of fertilizer contains a set of numbers that tells the amount of the three major nutrients provided by that fertilizer. A bag marked 6–24–24, for example, provides 6% nitrogen (N), 24% phosphorus (P), and 24% potassium (K). Your local nursery person can explain more about this method of labeling.

Test the effect of various fertilizers on plant growth. Divide your model plot into nine sections. Fill each section with the same kind of soil. Plant six radish seeds in each section. Then add ⅛ teaspoon of each of the following to one of the sections:

1. No fertilizer.

2. High in N; no P or K.

3. High in P; no N or K.

4. High in K; no N or P.

5. High in N and P; no K.

6. High in N and K; no P.

7. High in P and K; no N.

8. High in N, P, and K.

9. Chicken manure.

Note: Ask your nursery worker for samples of each of the above fertilizers. You could also talk with this person about the proper way to apply the fertilizer to the soil in your model plot.

Keep a record of the way the seeds sprout and the way plants grow in each of these sections. After the plants have four leaves each, write a brief statement that describes the size, color, and shape of each plant. Based on your research, write a report that summarizes the effects of various fertilizers on the growth of radishes.

Do other types of plants respond the same way to these fertilizers? Do the patterns of plant growth you observed in the first two weeks continue as the plants grow larger? What is the effect on plant growth of increasing the amount of each type of fertilizer by two, three, or more times? Do other kinds of manure have the same effect on plant growth as does chicken manure? Devise projects that will allow you to answer one or more of these questions.

Some people are concerned about the widespread use of chemical fertilizers in modern agriculture. For example, long-term use of chemical fertilizers seems to destroy the natural fertility of soil. Make a list of other disadvantages of using chemical fertilizers. You should talk with a nursery worker, a farmer, a county extension agent, or a biology or agriculture teacher. You should also refer to textbooks in environmental science and current magazine articles on this topic. Try to devise a project that will allow you to examine firsthand one or more of the objections to the use of chemical fertilizers you hear about.

Modern agriculture would be better off, some critics say, if more natural fertilizers and fewer chemical fertilizers were used to grow crops. Refer to the resources mentioned above for more information on this suggestion. Then design a project that will allow you to compare the advantages and disadvantages of natural and chemical fertilizers.

IRRIGATION

All plants need water to grow. In many parts of the world, rainfall does not provide enough water to grow crops, so water is brought to farmland from lakes and rivers that are miles—sometimes many miles—away. The process by which water is transported and delivered to farmland is called irrigation.

In the most common method of irrigation, water travels from a source to fields in open canals. Farmers take water from the canals to water their crops using giant sprinklers or smaller canals.

You can construct a model irrigation system in your model plot. Make the irrigation canal from any material that can be shaped into a half-cylinder. For example, you

In one of the most common methods
of irrigation, water is directed to crop rows
by means of canals and channels.

could form a long, narrow piece of stiff plastic into a gut-ter-shaped canal. Or you could use aluminum soft drink cans to make the canal. Cut the top and bottom off a can and then cut the can in half the long way. You will then have two half-cylinders that can be joined to make a short irrigation ditch. Using other cans, you can make the model ditch as long as you like. Think of other meth-ods for making a model irrigation ditch of other materials and of other sizes.

Install your model irrigation ditch along the long side of your model plot. Seal it at both ends so that it will hold water. Then fill the ditch with a measured amount of water.

One of the problems with irrigation systems is that so much water is lost by evaporation. Find a way to calculate the amount of water lost from your ditch after one day and again after one week. Using these data, calculate the amount of water lost from a real irrigation ditch that is 10 m wide and 10 km long.

Now put your irrigation system into operation. Figure out a way by which water can be transferred from the irrigation ditch to your model plot. Plant radish seeds throughout the model plot. Use irrigation water only to keep the radish plants alive.

How efficient is your irrigation system in delivering water to your plants? That is, what percentage of the water you put into the ditch is actually delivered to plants, and what percentage is lost by evaporation? Invent a method for calculating these percentages.

Think of ways to make your irrigation system more ef-ficient. For example, how do the size and shape of the irrigation canal affect its efficiency? Does it make any dif-ference how water is transferred from the ditch to the field?

How can you reduce the amount of irrigation water lost by evaporation? You can probably think of some ob-vious solutions with your model canal. But will those solu-tions work and will they be practical with real systems? Write a paper that recommends one or more ways in which this problem might be solved in the real world. Use your own project results to support your recommendations.

ENVIRONMENTAL PROBLEMS FROM FARMLAND RUNOFF

Modern agricultural techniques have vastly improved agricultural efficiency. But those techniques have also created problems for society. One set of problems arises as a result of the runoff from farmlands.

Chemicals are widely used on farmlands for two purposes: as fertilizers and as poisons to kill pests (pesticides) and weeds (herbicides). When these chemicals enter the soil, they can create environmental problems.

Fertilizers, pesticides, and herbicides become part of the environment in one of two ways. First, they may soak into the soil, enter the underground water system, and be transported to a nearby lake or river. Second, they may be washed off the surface of the ground into a nearby lake or river.

You can study the movement of agricultural chemicals with your model plot. To do so, you will need to learn how to test for certain chemicals in fertilizers. (Testing for pesticides and herbicides is too complex and will not be discussed here.) You can learn about methods of testing in one of three ways:

1. Many companies make kits for testing water quality. You can find a partial list of those companies in the appendix. Obtain a testing kit from one of these companies and follow the directions provided with the kit. Work with your adult partner on these tests.

2. Ask a science teacher, a worker at your local water or health department, a county extension agent, or another adult with experience to explain tests for agricultural chemicals. Then work with that adult in carrying out those tests.

3. Follow the directions given below for some typical tests.

AGRICULTURAL CHEMICALS IN
SUBSURFACE WATER

Plant about a dozen mature plants in your model plot. Any kind of flower or vegetable will be satisfactory. Select a fertilizer that has at least 20 percent of each major component (N, P, and K) in it (a 20–20–20 or better product). The fertilizer must contain some nitrogen in the form of nitrate.

Apply the fertilizer to the model plot as directed on the package. Then water the plot until the soil is soaked. Immediately collect any water that drains out of the bottom into the tray below the plot. Filter the water until it is clear and store it in a stoppered bottle. Label the bottle with the date and time the sample was collected.

Water the plot again 24 hours later. Soak the soil and collect the water that drains into the tray. Again filter the water and store it in a stoppered, labeled bottle. Repeat the process every 24 hours for at least one week. As soon as possible after collecting a sample, test the run-through water for one or more components of the fertilizer. Use a commercial test kit or one of the tests for phosphorus, nitrogen, and potassium given below.

For the following **three** tests, work under the supervision of a qualified **science teacher.**

Test for Phosphorus (in the Form of Phosphate)

Safety Notes
1. Wear safety goggles, gloves, and a lab coat or lab apron while doing this project.

2. Dilute sulfuric acid is toxic and can burn your skin and clothing. Use it with care. If you spill any on yourself, wash it off with water.

3. Ammonium molybdate is slightly toxic. If you spill any on yourself, wash it off well with water.

In a 250-mL flask, dissolve 1 g of sodium phosphate in 100 mL of distilled water. To 10 mL of this solution, add 5 drops of dilute (6N) sulfuric acid, 1 mL of 10% ammonium molybdate solution, and a small piece of tin. (In place of the tin, you can use a small piece of a vitamin C tablet.)

Stir the solution well and watch for a color change. To hasten the reaction, you can place the flask in a container of warm water. The color change you see is an indication of the presence of phosphorus in the form of phosphate.

Make successively more dilute solutions of sodium phosphate in water. For example, take 1 mL of the original solution and dilute it with 10 mL of water. Then dilute 1 mL of the original solution with 100 mL of water. Make other dilutions until you have six solutions of different dilutions. Repeat the above test on each diluted solution. Compare the colors produced in each of these solutions.

Repeat the above test on the run-through water samples you collected from the model plot. Compare the color of your run-through samples with the known samples you prepared. How does the amount of phosphate in the run-through samples change over time? What information does this provide you about the fate of the fertilizer you added to the model plot?

Find a way to estimate the amount of phosphate in the run-through water samples. Then estimate the percentage of fertilizer added to the model plot that washed away into the subsurface water.

Test for Nitrogen (in the Form of Nitrate)

Safety Notes
1. Wear safety goggles, gloves, and a lab coat or lab apron during this project.

2. Diphenylamine is toxic. The diphenylamine solution contains concentrated sulfuric acid, which is toxic and very corrosive. Handle the solution with care. If you spill any on your skin, wash it off with water.

3. Sodium nitrate is toxic. If you spill any on yourself, wash thoroughly with water.

In a 250-mL flask, dissolve 1 g of sodium nitrate in 100 mL of water. To 10 mL of this solution, add 10 drops of diphenylamine solution that your teacher has prepared for you. Watch for a color change. The color change you see indicates the presence of nitrate in the solution.

Make solutions of varying dilutions as you did for the phosphate test. Repeat the diphenylamine test with each of these solutions. These tests will show you what the diphenylamine test with various concentrations of nitrate will look like. Then test the run-through water samples for nitrate. Try to find a way to estimate the amount of nitrate in each run-through sample and the percentage of nitrate that washed into subsurface water.

Test for Potassium

Safety Notes

1. Wear safety goggles, gloves, and a lab coat or lab apron during this project.

2. Nitric acid is toxic and can burn your skin and clothing. Handle it with care. If you spill any on yourself, wash it off with water.

3. Potassium nitrate and sodium cobaltnitrite are toxic. If you spill any on yourself, wash thoroughly with water.

In a 250-mL flask, dissolve 1 g of potassium nitrate in 100 mL of water. To 10 mL of this solution, add 5 drops of dilute

(1N) nitric acid and 10 drops of sodium cobaltnitrite. Stir the solution with a glass stirring rod and let it set for about 5 minutes. The yellow precipitate that forms indicates the presence of potassium.

Make solutions of varying dilutions as you did for the phosphate and nitrogen tests. Repeat the sodium cobalt-nitrite test with each of these solutions to see what the test will look like with various concentrations of potassium. Then test the run-through water sample for potassium. Can you estimate the amount of potassium in each run-through sample and the percentage of potassium that washes into subsurface water?

AGRICULTURAL CHEMICALS
IN SURFACE RUNOFF

If farmland is hilly, some agricultural chemicals will wash off the surface of the soil. You can test this effect by elevating one end of your model plot. Place a pair of bricks under one end of the plot. Devise a method for collecting water that runs off the surface of the soil at the lower end.

Prepare the model plot with plants and fertilizer as in the previous project. Water the plants enough so that some water runs off the surface into the drain you have prepared at the lower end of the model plot. Capture and filter that water. Collect it in a stoppered bottle that is labeled with the date and time of collection. Repeat this process once every 24 hours for at least one week.

As soon as possible after each collection, test the run-off water for nitrogen, phosphorus, and potassium with your test kit or by another method approved by your adult partner. As before, try to estimate the percentage of fertilizer that washes off the land after one day, two days, three days, and so on. What is the total loss of fertilizer by both surface and subsurface runoff?

Various factors may affect the rate of surface runoff. For example, runoff might be greater from land with a steeper slope. The amount, duration, and timing of rainfall might also affect the rate of runoff. What other factors might be important? How important are these factors in loss of fertilizer from the land? Devise one or more projects that will answer these questions.

THE EFFECTS OF AGRICULTURAL CHEMICALS ON LIVING ORGANISMS

Agricultural chemicals can be very beneficial to growing plants, but they can also be harmful to organisms in the soil and water around the plants. In this project, you can observe the effects of some agricultural chemicals on organisms.

You could use any number of organisms for this project. For example, you can buy brine shrimp eggs at most pet stores. When added to water, these eggs hatch within a few days to produce larvae. You can observe the behavior of these larvae with the naked eye, with a magnifying glass, or with a microscope. A biology teacher will be able to suggest—and even provide you with—other organisms that can be used in this project.

Establish a healthy culture of the organism you have chosen to use for this project. Make sure they have a source of food, such as a few drops of yeast solution, every day. After the culture has been established, divide it into about a dozen jars. Each jar can be used to test one kind of fertilizer or some other factor of interest.

For example, choose a particular type of fertilizer to work with, perhaps a 10–10–10 type. Dissolve 1 g of fertilizer in 1 L of water. Add 10 drops of this solution to one jar of your culture. After 10 minutes, check to see if the fertilizer has had any effect on the organisms. Examine the organisms every 10 minutes until you see no further change or until you think no change will occur.

Then, 24 hours later, add 10 drops more of the fertilizer solution to the same jar. Check your organisms every 10 minutes as you did before. Continue this process once a day for at least one week. Keep a careful record of any changes you see in the culture.

You may find that your fertilizer solution is too strong or too weak. All the organisms may die within a few minutes or after the first day. Or you may see no change at all after one full week. Try changing the concentration of your fertilizer solution to get changes you can monitor over a period of about a week.

When you obtain some data on the amount of fertilizer needed to kill the organisms at a controlled rate, think of other factors you can test. For example, are nitrogen, phosphorus, and potassium all equally harmful to organisms? Are some organisms more susceptible to damage by fertilizer than others? How does the loss of organisms in a lake or river affect, if at all, other organisms that live in the lake or river? Devise one or more projects that will help you answer questions like these.

4

LAND AND WATER USE

Like most other topics in this book, issues of land and water use are fairly new in the history of the United States. A century ago, most Americans would have chuckled at the idea that people would be fighting over land and natural resources. The United States is one of the largest, most richly endowed nations in the world. Our ancestors could probably never have imagined that we would run out of either land or the resources it provides.

But that is just what is happening. Our population continues to grow, but our land resources remain constant. As a result, debates over the best use of those limited land resources have become more and more common. It is commonplace today to hear debates about how best to use rich farmlands, wetlands, lands that border oceans and lakes, land within cities, forests and prairies, and just about every other type of land resource you can imagine.

Similar disputes concern the use of water resources. In many parts of the nation today, farmers, city dwellers, industrialists, and conservationists are fighting with each other about how to use our limited water resources. The projects in this chapter will help you better understand land and water use questions that face your community, the nation, and the world.

NATURAL EROSION

We tend to think of land as a fixed resource that we can always count on. But, in fact, soil is constantly being lost. It washes away in rain storms, is blown away by winds, and is carried away by ocean currents.

You can use the model plot described on page 35 to study loss of land by running water. Elevate one end of the model plot with a pair of bricks. If your model plot has holes at the bottoms of its sides, seal them well. Provide an area at the lower end of the model plot where water can collect to form a miniature lake. Be ready to provide an overflow from the lake if it gets too high for the lower wall of the model plot.

Now you can test various factors involved in land erosion using the model. The most basic project is to observe the rate and character of erosion when rain falls on soil in the model plot. You can simulate rain by pouring water on the soil with a watering can. But, with a little thought, you can probably develop more sophisticated methods of simulating rain. For example, try to find nozzles at a local hardware store that will spray water on the soil in a fine mist.

With this setup, you can observe the effect of "natural" rainfall on a "natural" piece of land over a period of time. The observations you make of this simple system will provide a baseline against which you can compare later projects.

Find a way to estimate the amount or percentage of soil lost during this project. You should be able to make a statement such as:

Land is constantly being washed away by
storms, winds, and ocean currents.

"1000 mL of water falling on 10 square meters of land with a slope of 5° results in a loss of 5 g (0.1%) of soil from the land."

Consider some simple changes that can be made in this basic project. For example, how do your results change when you use different kinds of soil in your model plot? How does the slope of the land affect the amount and rate of erosion? How does the topography (shape and smoothness of the surface) affect erosion? Does the rate and pattern of rainfall have any effect on erosion patterns?

You should be able to write a new statement about the rate of erosion for each factor you test. You can then compare these new statements with the original statement above.

Think about land erosion in your community. Are there places in the community that look like your model plot? Chances are there are not. Instead, your environment is likely to contain other natural objects (trees, bushes, grass, etc.) as well as human-made structures (roads, farms, buildings, etc.).

Make any change in your model plot that will simulate any one of these factors. For example, you could cover all or part of the soil in your model plot with sod. Then you could determine how the kind, location, thickness, and other properties of grass affect soil erosion.

Next, add a second element to your model plot. For example, you could install plants that would simulate trees and bushes. Your model plot should begin to look more like a natural landscape on which humans have had no impact. Devise a project that will allow you to determine how erosion occurs in such an area and the way each individual factor in the environment affects the rate of erosion. Again, try to write one or more statements about the rate of erosion for each factor you test.

Look for an area in your community that corresponds to the model you made above. A city, state, or national park might be such an area. How closely does the natural area match the characteristics of your model plot project?

EROSION CAUSED BY
HUMAN ACTIVITIES

Now look for ways in which humans have changed the natural environment. (See page 54). What examples can you find in which structures or human behaviors have changed the appearance of the natural area? Can you simulate some of these human effects in your model plot?

For example, what is the effect of placing a parking lot on one section of your model plot? An office building? An artificial pond? What is the effect of building a road across the model plot? Along the length of it? Again, you should be able to determine the amount of soil lost because of each factor you test. Summarize each of your findings in a "Rate of Erosion" statement.

You should have no trouble finding examples of erosion caused by humans in your community. Find an adult partner who is willing to survey the community with you. Perhaps you can ask someone from the city engineer's office, the county environmental protection agency, the state highway department, the U.S. Corps of Engineers, or another person interested in land erosion to be your partner. In any case, you should be able to get additional information about land erosion in the community from such a person.

In your community survey, take photographs of land that is undergoing erosion. Try to find out what human activities have resulted in the erosion. Think about the benefits of those activities in comparison with the harm they

The paved road and suburban-style homes
built on farmland are common sights all
across the United States. In many areas,
homes are being built as quickly as
farmland is sold to developers.

may cause. For example, is land erosion around a new school site a reasonable price to pay for having the new school? Look for ways in which land erosion could be avoided, reduced, or corrected.

Other natural forces can also cause soil erosion. For example, in some parts of the United States and in other countries, winds blow away large amounts of valuable topsoil. Devise one or more projects that will allow you to test the effects of wind erosion.

Begin with the basic model plot that contains soil and no vegetation or other elements. Use a fan or some other method to simulate the wind. Find a method to collect soil blown off the model plot by the wind. See how soil loss is related to wind velocity. Then make changes in your model plot, as you did for the running water projects, adding various types of vegetation and human-built structures.

Find out why soil erosion by wind is or is not an important problem in your community. Devise and, with your model plot, test a method for reducing the loss of topsoil by wind.

LAND USE

One of the most familiar questions facing communities today is how best to use their lands. Vacant land is often a rare commodity. When land does become available, many groups want to use it for their own purposes. In many cases, each possible use—for homes, a new factory, recreational purposes, etc.—is legitimate, important, and valuable.

For this project, find an unused piece of land in or near your community. It could be a vacant lot, an abandoned factory site, an old railroad yard, an abandoned dock, an undeveloped forest, or another piece of land. Your task is to decide how best to use the land.

To complete this task, you need to answer a number of specific questions. Those questions fall into three major areas:

A dust storm in the United States
is as likely to blow away topsoil
as is this storm in India.

1. What are the characteristics of the land? How large is it? Does it have access to water? Are utilities (electricity, telephone, etc.) available to it?

2. What legal restrictions apply to the land? Is it zoned for a specific purpose or purposes? Is it protected by special laws such as those in a historic district? Who owns the land?

3. What are the potential uses for the land? Who would like to buy the land and for what purpose? What are the advantages of using the land for (1) new housing, (2) light industry, (3) an office building, (4) recreation, (5) open (undeveloped) space, (6) any other use you can think of? What are the disadvantages of each possible use?

Deciding how to use this land can become a large project. You may want to get some help from friends who are interested in this topic. In some schools, classes have devoted a whole year to answering some or all of the above questions.

You will need to get a lot of information and expert advice on this project. A visit to the local zoning board and to the city planning office is essential. You will also need to interview individuals and groups who have an interest in the piece of land. People who live near the land will have opinions about the way it should and should not be used.

Based on your research, write a proposal that tells how you think this piece of land ought to be used. If and when the question of developing the land comes up, you may be able to present and defend your proposal.

LAND USE IN YOUR COMMUNITY

Obtain a map that shows how land in your community is being used today and how it was used thirty years ago. Your local zoning office and the local library will probably have such maps. Make a photocopy of each map. Then color each one to show the ways land is and was used. You could use yellow for residential areas, for example, green for office space, red for industrial areas, blue for farms, white for transportation systems, purple for parks and open spaces, and so on.

Compare the two maps. How has land use in the community changed over thirty years? What factors have brought about these changes? In what respects do the changes represent an improvement in the community's quality of life?

What will your community look like thirty years from now? You have just analyzed the forces that brought about the development of the community in which you now live. Will those forces continue to make similar changes in the future?

Make a third map that shows what you think the community should look like in thirty years. The map should highlight past improvements that should be retained and continued, past errors that should be corrected, future needs that must be met, and general improvements in the community's quality of life.

Based on the map you have just drawn, prepare a set of planning recommendations for the community. What planning decisions must the community take now in order to have the "ideal" community you envision thirty years from now?

WATER USE IN YOUR COMMUNITY

You have seen that land-use decisions are important in many communities today. In many places, obtaining adequate supplies of fresh water can also be a problem. In most of the southwestern states, for example, water use has become as much of an issue as land use. Between 1987 and 1990, for example, most of California received

**Drought in California lowered the level
of this lake and left the ground parched.**

much less rainfall and snowfall than normal. In the last three of the decade, water rationing was in effect in much of our nation's most populous state.

As in much of California, many communities are building housing for new residents, increasing farm irrigation, and trying to capture new industries—all activities that require fresh water—in spite of the fact that water resources are not increasing and, in fact, are running low in those same areas. In this section, you can carry out a series of projects to learn more about the water resources in your own community.

YOUR WATER RESOURCES

Where does the water your community uses come from? How much water is normally available from these sources? How has this volume of water changed over the last twenty years? What are predictions for the availability of water from these sources in the next twenty years?

What kind of treatment does water receive before it reaches your community? What is the cost of this treatment? How has water treatment and its cost changed in the recent past? How are they expected to change in the near future?

Answers to questions such as these will give you some ideas about water resources now available to your community. Talk with someone in your local water department about the answers to these questions. You may want to do a general survey of the issue of water resources in your community. If you choose to do so, you may be able to find other teenagers or adults who will work with you on this project.

Or you might want to choose just one of the above questions and do a detailed study. For example, suppose you want to study in detail the second question, "How much water is normally available from your community's water source(s)?" You could learn how these water resources are actually measured. You could try to find records of water reserves from the past. You could analyze how these reserves have changed over time. Any one of the questions in the first two paragraphs of this section can be expanded to provide a complete project on that topic.

In any case, you should be able to prepare a report on all or one part of the community's water resources. This report is a necessary first step in analyzing water-use problems your community will face in the future.

WATER USE IN THE COMMUNITY

Now you know how much water is available to your community. Is it enough for the community's needs this year? Next year? In 10 years? In 20 years?

Talk with an adult partner at the water department. Find out how much water the community used last year. How much was used by agriculture? By industry? By private homes? How does the amount of water used compare to the amount of water available? Based on your analysis, does your community seem to have a water-use problem?

What is the outlook for the future? Does the water department have projections for future water needs in the community? Is the community's water situation going to get worse? Get better? Remain unchanged?

Arrange for interviews with the city planning director, the school board's planning office, representatives of industry and agriculture, private developers, and others in the community about their plans for the near future. Are the city water department's plans and projections for the future realistic?

Based on these interviews, decide what you think the city's water future is for the next decade. Prepare a report that describes what actions, if any, the community should take to assure itself of an adequate water supply in the near future.

CONSERVING WATER

Water conservation is important in most communities for one of two reasons. First, there may not be enough water to supply community needs now and in the future. Second, even if there is enough water, purifying water for community use is becoming more and more expensive. (Why?) Thus, most communities in the United States can benefit from finding ways to conserve water. Here are some projects that deal with water conservation in your community.

WATER CONSERVATION AT HOME

Most families use more water than they need to. To see if this applies to your home, make an audit of water use by your family. First, make a list of ways your family uses water. Then estimate the amount of water used (in gallons) for each purpose each day. Table 3 is a possible format for the information you gather. (Do not write in the book.)

Add other ways in which water is used in your home. Then determine how much water is used for each activity. Multiply the number of times each activity occurs in one day and in one week. Calculate the amount of water used in the household each day and each week.

One source of water use may be leaks. See if you have any leaky pipes or faucets. If so, put a bucket under the leak and determine the amount of water lost from the leak per day and per week.

Suppose your family were required to reduce its water consumption by 25 percent. Use the chart to determine where those savings could be made. Make a list of the ways you could save enough water to meet this requirement. Your local water department may have additional suggestions.

TABLE 3. SAMPLE WATER AUDIT CHART

Use	Amount of Water Used	Number of Times per Day	Water Use per Day	Number of Times per Week	Water Use per Week
showers					
tooth-brushing					
shaving					
toilet flushing					
dish washing					
car washing					
garden/ lawn watering					
cooking					
clothes washing					

SAMPLE

WATER CONSERVATION
IN THE COMMUNITY

In many communities, only a small fraction of all water used goes to private homes. In California, for example, 85 percent of all water is used by agriculture. The remaining 15 percent goes to residential, industrial, and all other uses. That means that even the most conscientious program of water conservation by private citizens will have only a modest effect on water use in some areas.

Find out how other users in your community conserve water. Visit any one of the following and interview the owner, manager, or person in charge of water use. Find out what water conservation practices are now in use and what practices are planned for the future.

1. Local factory.

2. Office building.

3. Restaurant.

4. School district.

5. Farm.

6. Local electric company.

7. Athletic stadium.

8. City park, zoo, public garden, or other outdoor facility.

Include in the list any other building or operation in which large amounts of water may be used. If possible, try to interview people from a number of locations on the list. The more people you talk with, the better you will be able to assess your community's water use and water conservation practices.

From information provided by the person(s) you interview, try to estimate how much water the building, business, industry, farm, or facility will be able to conserve. Would

they be able to meet the same 25 percent savings requirement that is imposed on private homes? At the con-
clusion of this project, you should be able to prepare a
set of recommendations for water conservation in your
community.

5

SOLID WASTES

A major problem in the United States today is what to do with solid wastes. Each day, Americans produce an average of 53 kg of waste. About 90 percent of these wastes come from agriculture and mining operations. Another 6 percent is produced by industry, and 4 percent by communities and private households.

On this scale, community wastes seem like a small problem. But they are not. Many communities have run out of places to dump their solid wastes. Some communities pay huge sums of money to ship their wastes dozens or hundreds of kilometers away for disposal. As landfills and dumps become full, more and more communities will face similar problems. The projects in this chapter will outline some of the issues involved in the management of solid wastes.

The United States and other nations have solid waste problems for three reasons. First, they are inclined to throw away materials and objects rather than to repair and reuse them. Second, many of these discarded materials do not break down very quickly. Thus, mountains of trash tend to accumulate rapidly. Third, some of the discarded materials are hazardous to plants, animals, and humans.

The first set of projects describes some activities related to the problem of wastes not breaking down quickly.

MEASURING THE RATE OF DECAY

How fast do various waste materials decay? Here is a project that will help you answer that question. Select a variety of typical waste materials. Begin with a sheet of newspaper, a plastic soda bottle, an empty aluminum can, the skin of an orange, a piece of wood, an elastic (rubber) band, a square of cotton or wool cloth, a square of nylon, rayon, polyester, or other synthetic fabric, a piece of plastic wrap, a styrofoam food container, and three or four dead leaves. Include any other waste materials from your own garbage or trash can.

Get an aquarium that holds at least 10 gallons. Fill the aquarium halfway with soil. Place your waste samples on top of the soil, along the sides of the aquarium. You must be able to see these samples through the aquarium glass. Finally, cover the samples with about 15 cm of dirt.

Place the aquarium where you can observe it on a regular basis. Water the soil every day or two. Make sure the soil is moist, but not soggy. Make a record of any changes you see in the aquarium. Which materials decay fastest? Which decay very slowly, or not at all?

You will have to develop a way to measure the decay. You may be able to make some decisions just by looking through the aquarium glass. But you may also want to develop more detailed tests. You could begin with more than one piece of each sample and more than one aquarium. Then you could observe one aquarium and perform tests on samples from the other aquarium. What tests would be helpful in determining the rate of decay?

Think of variations on this project. For example, does

it make any difference how large the samples are? Do ten 5-cm squares of paper decay at the same rate as one 50-cm square? How does moisture affect the rate of decay? Do all materials decay faster when the ground is very wet or very dry? Or does moisture affect materials in different ways? Does temperature or light affect the rate of decay? Develop variations on the original procedure outlined above to answer these questions.

Devise other variations on this project. You could find out, for example, if the rate of decay depends on whether materials are exposed to the air. Repeat the original project with your samples sitting on top of the dirt in the aquarium. Does the rate of decay depend on whether these samples are kept moist or dry? Does sunlight or temperature have any effect on the rate of decay?

Try to think of factors that humans can control that might affect the rate of decay. For example, suppose you could find a way to pass air through the soil. Would that change the rate of decay for some or all materials? How could you build and test a device for moving air through the soil? What other factors can you think of trying?

One solution proposed for one aspect of the solid waste problem is biodegradable plastic containers. Some manufacturers have produced a form of plastic that, they say, will decompose once it is discarded. Obtain one or more samples of plastic labeled "biodegradable." Find the rate of decay of these samples when exposed to the air; when buried underground; when exposed to sunlight; when left in the dark; when stored in a moist environment; when

How long do you think the materials in this city dump in southeastern Massachusetts will take to decompose and revert back to woodland?

kept dry. Prepare a report that compares the biodegradability of these samples to that of other plastics, paper, and other materials you test.

YOUR SHARE OF THE PROBLEM

How much does your own family contribute to your community's solid waste problem? Here are some ideas for finding the answer to this question.

For one week, volunteer to become Waste Management Specialist for your household. Work out a system by which all household solid wastes are saved, packaged, and labeled by type. For example, you could get five large plastic trash bags. All paper products could go into one bag, all glass products into a second bag, all metal products into a third bag, all plastic products into a fourth bag, and all garbage (waste food) into a fifth bag. Be considerate of other family members and store your containers in an out-of-the-way place. **Caution:** Wear protective gloves and watch out for sharp objects.

At the end of the week, weigh the amount of waste in each bag. This weight tells you how much your family contributes to the community's solid waste problems each week. How much do they contribute in one year? Assume your family is typical of others in the community. What is the total amount of each kind of waste produced in your community in one week? In one year?

Combine your results from this project with your results from the Rate of Decay projects above. How could you change your family's waste disposal practices to help solve the community's waste disposal problems? For example, what changes in household practices would produce more wastes that decay rapidly and fewer wastes that decay more slowly? Make a list of those changes and try them out for one week. What changes in the amount of wastes of each kind do you find?

As you collect various types of wastes, make a list of

objects that are discarded because they can no longer be used. Some examples of these objects would be a broken plastic cup, a metal tool with one part missing, a burned-out light bulb, a bent curtain rod, a radio that no longer works, and a cracked flowerpot.

What could be done to make this list smaller? That is, how can your family (and your community) find ways to (1) make objects of sturdier materials, (2) repair damaged objects, and (3) otherwise extend the life of these "throwaways"?

Decide whether changes like these would help solve your community's solid waste problems. To make this decision, you may want to talk with people who make or sell these objects. For example, ask a hardware person about the relative cost of repairing a tool versus buying a new one; about the relative cost of using a long-life light bulb versus an ordinary bulb; about repairing a radio versus buying a new one. What are the economic and other factors that make the United States a "throwaway" society, and what are the chances that this philosophy can be changed?

Consider finding new uses for discarded objects. For example, you might be able to use a cracked flowerpot to hold nails in the workshop. What other creative uses can you think of for discarded objects and materials?

INVESTIGATING BUSINESS WASTES

Private homes are only one source of solid wastes. Businesses and industries also contribute to the community's solid waste problems

---

Safety Notes

Trash areas contain many materials that are potentially dangerous, including broken glass, sharp pieces of metal, and disease-causing organisms. Wear protective

gloves (for example, plastic gloves), a lab coat or other protective clothing, and a face mask. Be sure to work under the supervision of an adult.

Locate one business that will allow you to do a study of wastes for one week, one day, or one hour. For example, you could ask a local fast-food restaurant to let you check some or all of their trash cans every hour for one day. You can use a trash-collecting and labeling method similar to the one that you used in your own home. How does the amount of paper, plastic, glass, metal, and other wastes from this business compare with the amount produced by your own family?

Some agency in your city government will also have information on solid wastes in the community. For example, you could interview someone in the city sanitation department or the private company that picks up trash in your community. Find out where the largest volume of trash comes from: private homes, businesses, factories, farms, or other sources. Are some kinds of businesses, factories, and farms more of a problem than others? Why?

How much trash does your community have to dispose of each day? How much of that trash is paper? Glass? Metal? Garbage? Other kinds of waste?

Prepare an illustrated report that shows what you learned in this project about your community's solid waste problems. What are the sources and composition of those wastes?

Colonel Sanders' recipe for fast-food fried chicken also seems to be a recipe for fast-food trash problems.

DOWN IN THE DUMPS

Another way to understand your community's solid waste problems is to visit a local garbage dump and study its content.

Safety Notes

Dumps contain many materials that are potentially dangerous: broken glass, sharp pieces of metal, and disease-causing organisms. Wear plastic gloves, a lab coat or other protective clothing, and a face mask when you work in the dump. Also, do this project only when accompanied by an adult partner.

Ask the dump operator to let you study a small section of the dump. Find a way to estimate the percentage of each kind of waste material (paper, plastic, glass, metal, etc.) in the section you study. How do those percentages compare with the percentages of different kinds of wastes from your own home? From the business you studied? From the estimates provided by the person you interviewed?

Talk with the dump operator about your findings. How has the character of the dump changed in the past five years or more? What problems most concern the dump operator about solid waste disposal? How are those problems likely to change in the near future?

Also find out what kind of dump(s) your community has. Is the dump you studied a sanitary landfill or some other kind of dump? What problems with leakage has the dump experienced in the past?

Communities sometimes have "unofficial" dumps. For one reason or another, people decide to throw their trash into one of those public areas. A common example is the area alongside a road or highway. People often seem to think that it is acceptable to throw trash out their car win-

This scene resembles the dump in
an earlier picture, but it is actually a
section of a highway in Florida.

dows. Vacant lots, school grounds, beaches, and public parks also may contain unofficial dumps.

Safety Notes

Follow the safety warning in the previous project.

Select one of these areas in your community to study. If you select a road or highway, or some other dangerous area, ask an adult partner to go with you. Pick up all the trash in a certain portion of that area, for example, along a half-kilometer (quarter-mile) stretch of the highway. Separate the trash according to type: paper, plastic, glass, metal, etc.; and/or according to function: bottles, boxes, bags, etc.

How does the composition of trash in this unofficial dump compare with trash from your own household? From the business you studied? What hints, if any, does the composition of this trash give you about ways to reduce solid waste disposal in this area? Devise a plan that may reduce the dumping of trash in the area you studied.

RECYCLING

An earlier project in this chapter suggested ways for you to think about the throwaway mentality of our society. Another way to deal with that mentality is through recycling. Many of the materials Americans throw out can be recycled, that is, used again. Among these are some kinds of metal, glass, and paper.

To understand the potential for recycling, you first need to find out what kinds of materials can and cannot be recycled. Your community probably has a public or private agency that handles recycling. Interview a knowledgeable person at that agency. Get a list of the kinds of materials the agency can and cannot accept. Find out what materials are and are not recyclable.

Many communities throughout the United
States have centers such as this one where
trash can be brought and recycled.

During your interview, you may also want to learn about the community's recycling program. How effective is that program, that is, what fraction of potential recyclable materials are actually collected? Is the program becoming more or less successful? Is it profitable? What does the attitude of people in the community seem to be toward recycling?

Now try to estimate the potential for recycling in the trash from your own household. By what fraction could your solid wastes be reduced by sorting out newspapers, bottles, cans, and other recyclable objects? Make a similar estimate for the business trash you studied in the project above.

The success of recycling programs depends on public support. How do your friends and neighbors feel about recycling? Do they think it is a good idea? Why or why not? Are they willing to participate in a recycling program? Why or why not? How can existing recycling programs in the community be expanded and/or improved? Prepare a questionnaire, and interview a sample of friends and neighbors to get answers to questions like these. Summarize your findings and present them to the local recycling agency.

6

ENERGY

Energy use is a critical feature of modern civilization. In fact, some authorities believe that the amount of energy a nation uses is a good measure of how "advanced" that nation is. In the United States, we use energy to operate cars, trucks, buses, trains, and airplanes; to heat and cool our homes and office buildings; to operate factories; and for many other purposes.

Most of the energy we use comes from the burning of coal, oil, and natural gas. Smaller amounts come from hydroelectric power and nuclear power plants as well as from geothermal wells, windmills, solar devices, and other alternative energy sources.

The United States faces two problems related to energy use. The first is the potential for serious shortages in the future. Our major energy sources—coal, oil, and natural gas—are all nonrenewable resources. When they are used up, they are essentially gone forever.

The second problem involves environmental effects. The burning of coal, oil, and natural gas releases waste products that contaminate the environment. For these two reasons, Americans must always be alert for better ways to produce and use energy. The projects in this chapter will introduce you to some of the issues surrounding energy use in our society.

A HOME ENERGY AUDIT

A good place to begin your study of energy is in your own home. How much energy does your family use and for what purposes? You probably use more than one form of energy in your home, perhaps gas for cooking and electricity for appliances, for example. It is often difficult to measure the amount of natural gas and oil used in the home. But an audit of electrical energy use is fairly easy.

First, make a list of all the places you use electricity in your home. The list might include items such as an oven, light bulbs, a stove, a toaster, a microwave oven, television sets, radios, and so on. The amount of energy used by each of these devices can be found from its "power rating," usually given in watts. You probably know, for example, that most light bulbs have power ratings of 40 watts, 75 watts, 100 watts, or some other value. Record the power rating of every appliance on your list. If you cannot find a power rating, use the average value given in Table 4. Then convert the power rating to kilowatts by dividing its value in watts by 1000.

Finally, count the number of hours each appliance is used each day. Compile a chart like Table 5, which shows how much electrical energy you use, and for what purposes, each day and each week.

You can calculate the amount of electrical energy used by multiplying the total power used by each appliance times the number of hours used. (The answer will be expressed in kilowatt-hours, or kwh.) What is the total amount of electrical energy used in your home each day? Each week?

TABLE 4. AVERAGE POWER RATING OF
CERTAIN ELECTRICAL APPLIANCES

Appliance	Power Rating (in watts)
Blender	300
Broiler	1000
Clock	5
Clothes dryer	5000
Dishwasher	1200
Electric blanket	200
Hair dryer	600
Iron	1000
Microwave oven	1200
Radio	75
Sunlamp	300
Television (color, solid state)	150
Washing machine	500
Water heater	2500
Window fan	200

Note. Ask your local electric company for power ratings of appliances not contained in this list.

You can also compare the relative amounts of various kinds of energy used in your home. One way to do that is to review your family's monthly energy bills. Those bills show how much money your family spends on oil, how much on natural gas, how much on electricity, and, perhaps, how much on coal. This information will allow you to calculate the *energy cost distribution.* For example, if your

TABLE 5. A SAMPLE HOME ENERGY AUDIT

Appliance

	Light Bulb	Microwave Oven
Number of Units	6	1
Power Rating per Unit	100 watts	500 watts
Total Power (in Watts)	600 watts	500 watts
Total Power (in Kilowatts)	0.6 kilowatts	0.5 kilowatts
Time Used per Day	30 hours*	1 hour
Time Used per Week	210 hours	7 hours
Energy Used per Day	18 kwh	0.5 kwh
Energy Used per Week	126 kwh	3.5 kwh

*Six bulbs, 5 hours per bulb.

energy bills show that your electrical charges last month were $52.89 and your gas charges were $46.17, then the percentage your family spent for each was as follows:

$$\text{For electricity: } \frac{\$52.89}{\$52.89 + \$46.17} \times 100\% = 53.4\%$$

$$\text{For gas: } \frac{\$46.17}{\$52.89 + \$46.17} \times 100\% = 46.6\%$$

You can also calculate the *amount distribution* by comparing the quantities of each source used. All you need to make this calculation is the following set of equivalences:

1000 cubic feet of gas = 7.6 gallons of oil = 293 kwh of electricity

On what forms of energy does your household depend? Which form is the most important? Which is the least important?

ENERGY USE IN BUSINESS AND INDUSTRY

About one quarter of all energy used in the United States is used in homes. Another quarter is used in transportation. The remaining half of our energy use is accounted for by factories (37 percent) and businesses (16 percent). How do business and industry in your community use energy?

You may be able to answer that question for a small company as you did for your own home. Locate a small business, shop, or factory whose owner will be willing to be interviewed. Try to get from that person information about his or her business energy use like that you obtained for your own household. That is, what kinds of energy does the business use? How much of each kind does it use? For what purposes is energy used in the business?

Perhaps you can find more than one business to study. Or you may be able to get friends to work with you and interview other types of businesses. In either case, you should be able to get a better idea of the way businesses and industries in your community use energy.

An additional topic to raise with the people you interview is the question of energy problems the company faces. Is there a problem of energy shortages, now or in the future, for this business? Have energy costs been a problem in the past? Are they now? Are they expected to be in the future? Does the company have any environmental problems associated with its use of energy? For example, does a local metal shop have to worry about air pollution because of the fuels it burns?

In your interview, one approach is to try to get an understanding of the overall picture of energy use in the business. A second approach is to look for and concentrate on a specific aspect of the company's use of energy. For example, the cost of energy, energy shortages, or pollution resulting from energy use may be an especially difficult problem for any one business. You could focus your questioning and research on that specific topic.

You will probably want to visit your local energy company for this project also. That way you can learn more about energy use in your community from the suppliers as well as from the consumers. Ask the energy company representative you talk with the same questions you asked the business owner. How much and what kind of energy does the company provide? How has energy production changed over the years? What changes are anticipated in the future? How does the energy company expect to deal with these future changes? What environmental problems does the energy company have to deal with? How is it doing so?

For your report you may want to focus on a single aspect of energy use in your community. For example, you could describe the way energy use in your community has changed over the past 50 years and the factors that account for those changes. Or you could summarize the way energy is now used in the community. Or you could compare energy use with energy production in the community and analyze any problems in this relationship. Or you could outline the future of energy use and production in the community. Finally, you could outline environmental problems associated with energy use in the community and propose ways in which those problems ought to be resolved.

ENERGY CONSERVATION

Many people agree that Americans use more energy than they need to. What are some of the ways energy can be conserved in your own home? In the business(es) you studied? In the community at large?

Review the analysis of energy use in your household described on page 80. Examine the specific items on that list for possible places to cut down on energy use. For example, could you use fewer light bulbs or bulbs with lower wattage? Could you use the lights for fewer hours each day? Is it more efficient to use a microwave or a conventional oven?

Develop a plan that lists as many energy-saving steps as you can think of. Then put that plan into practice for one week. Do another energy audit, like the one described on page 82. Compare energy use before and after the conservation steps were taken.

Assess your conservation plan. Which steps were worthwhile and which were not? For example, did using fewer lights make it more difficult to read? Or did the house seem less safe because it was more dimly lit at night?

Talk with friends about your list of energy-saving steps. Which ones would probably work in their homes? What additional suggestions do they have to offer? Based on your own project and your conversations with friends, write an informational pamphlet on "Energy Conservation in the Home."

Energy conservation in business and industry may involve steps like those described in your pamphlet. But they are likely to also include other steps. Interview business owners about their efforts to conserve energy. You could include the subject of conservation in your original business and industry interviews (page 83).

Find out what things businesses have done to cut back on their use of energy. You should be able to come up with a list of specific suggestions such as adding insulation to the building, reducing the average room temperature in the building, and turning off lights at night.

Determine the advantages and disadvantages of each conservation technique you learn about. For example, you might discover that lowering room temperatures saves heating oil, but results in more illness among employees.

Based on the information obtained in these interviews, prepare a brochure on "Energy Savings Steps in Business and Industry" that summarizes your findings. Send copies of the brochure to companies in the community that might benefit from this information.

What is your local government doing about energy

conservation? Is there any community-wide program for reducing energy use? If so, how is information about the proram distributed? What has been the response of people and businesses in the community? Talk with your local energy company to obtain information on these questions.

THE PRIVATE AUTOMOBILE
AND ENERGY USE

Americans depend heavily on private automobiles for their transportation. Nearly two-thirds of all the petroleum used in the United States is burned as gasoline in private cars. Yet, cars are not a very efficient form of transportation. Furthermore, cars are the single most important source of air pollution in the United States. For these reasons, many people suggest that we find alternative ways of moving people within and between cities.

How can transportation within your community be improved? To answer that question, try to obtain as much background data as possible. Some questions you should try to answer are the following:

1. How many private automobiles are there in the community? How many registered drivers?

2. How much gasoline do these cars burn each year?

3. What environmental problems (for example, air pollution) do these cars produce and what is the extent of these problems?

4. What is the average number of passengers in each car?

5. What is the average distance traveled on each trip in a private car?

6. What is the average amount of energy used per person in private car travel?

You should be able to think of additional questions to add to this list.

Some of the information needed to answer these questions is available from public and private agencies. For example, the state department of vehicles should be able to answer question 1 for you. Local gasoline companies can help with 2. And the city environmental protection agency may have data on question 3. Public interest groups such as the Sierra Club, the League of Women Voters, Dallas Tomorrow, or Buffalo 2000 may be able to provide you with information.

You may be able to collect some useful data on your own. For example, stand on the corner of a busy intersection at various times of the day. Count the number of people in each car that passes the intersection. After just a few days, you may be able to estimate an answer for question 4.

You could also estimate the amount of gasoline wasted by private cars. For example, as you stand at an intersection, count the number of seconds each car remains at rest (for a stop sign, a traffic light, or because of congestion, for example). Call this "time wasted" because the cars were not moving. Then try to estimate the fraction of that time that was unavoidable (cars do have to stop at stop signs) and the fraction that was avoidable (maybe a four-way stop sign is not really necessary at this intersection).

Look for potential trouble spots—places where cars waste a lot of energy—to study. For example, does the timing of traffic lights on major streets contribute to or reduce the amount of time wasted by automobiles in the community?

Perhaps you will be able to observe a morning and/ or evening commute also. Try to estimate the fraction of time that cars are stopped because of congestion, accidents, or some other reason on a particular portion of the highway.

What other observations can you make that will allow

you to estimate the fraction of energy wasted by private cars in the community? Information collected for questions 1 through 6 plus your own questions will allow you to prepare a report on "The Private Car and Energy Use" in your community.

ALTERNATIVES TO THE PRIVATE CAR

In most communities, people do not have to travel by private car. Various forms of public transportation are available. To what extent is public transportation a real alternative in your community? What can be done to make it a more attractive option to people?

The first step in answering these questions is to learn more about your community's public transportation system. Some of the information you will need to collect includes the following:

1. How many people presently use public transportation each day?

2. What is the average number of riders per vehicle (bus, subway car, trolley car, etc.)?

3. What is the total amount of energy used by the public transportation system each year?

4. What is the average amount of energy used per rider in the system? (Compare this answer with the figure for private cars.)

5. How has ridership changed over the past 20 years?

6. What changes are likely to occur in the system in the next 20 years?

7. What factors prevent people from making greater use of public transportation?

Next, find out what people in your community want and expect from a public transportation system. Prepare a

Public transportation systems such
as Washington, D.C.'s subway help the
environment and economy in many ways,
including saving energy, reducing air
pollution, saving time, reducing traffic accidents,
and providing jobs.

questionnaire that you can use with friends and neighbors. Here are some of the questions you might want to ask:

1. How often do you use public transportation?
2. If you do use the system regularly,
   a. How would you rate the system: excellent, good, fair, or poor?
   b. What are the best features of the system?
   c. What are the worst features of the system?
   d. How could the system be improved?
3. If you do not use the system,
   a. Why not?
   b. What changes would have to be made to get you to use the system?

Add questions of your own if you like.

Try to interview at least ten people. See if some of your friends will also interview ten people each. Try to collect information from at least fifty people for this project. Make sure you have a good mixture of young and old, male and female, in your sample.

Based on your interviews, develop a proposal to submit to your community transportation system. The proposal should reflect (1) strengths of the present system, (2) complaints and suggestions from present riders and nonriders, (3) projections for future transportation needs, and (4) transportation technology that exists and is or is not used in the community.

To get information on item (4), talk with a representative of your local public transportation system or with your local librarian. You might also communicate with other communities that have developed successful forms of public transportation, such as Seattle's monorail, San Diego's Tijuana Trolley, and the "dial-a-ride" programs now available in many cities.

ALTERNATIVE ENERGY SOURCES

Some people are thinking about energy needs in the United States and the rest of the world twenty years or more into the future. At that point, our oil and natural gas reserves may be greatly diminished. What alternative sources of energy will we be able to turn to? Some possibilities include wind power, geothermal wells, nuclear power, and solar devices.

The utilization of most alternative energy sources depends to some extent on geographical factors. For example, geothermal power can be used only in regions where rocks heated by the earth's interior temperature lie fairly near the earth's surface. Residents of northern California, for example, get about 10 percent of their electricity from geothermal wells. But no such wells exist in most other regions of the United States.

What forms of alternative energy might be feasible in your community? You can get some basic information on this question from your local energy company. Or you may be able to find private companies that specialize in solar, wind, or other forms of energy. These experts will be able to show you how to determine which alternative energy sources can be used in your area.

For example, you could measure wind speed near your home with an anemometer borrowed from a local high school, college, or weather station. Use the anemometer to find the wind speed at three times during the day (10 A.M., 1 P.M., and 4 P.M., for example) every day for two weeks. Present these data to your adult partner at the local energy company or the alternative energy company. How much electrical energy can be generated with these wind patterns? How could that electrical energy be used in a home? In a business? In the community? How would the costs of wind energy compare with the present costs of electricity?

Instruments are available to measure the amount of

electricity generated by sunlight. Ask a science teacher about borrowing a device such as a solar energy meter. You can also purchase an instrument like this from one of the supply houses listed in the appendix.

Use the instrument to measure the amount of electricity produced by solar energy at your house every day for a period of two weeks. What practical use could be made of this amount of solar energy? How large would a device have to be to collect enough sunlight to use in a house? In a business? Ask your adult partner to illustrate solar equipment now available for heating water or for other residential or commercial uses.

Prepare a report that outlines the future potential of alternative energy sources in your community. What factors make the use of solar power, wind power, or other sources more or less likely in the next twenty years? What actions should the community take, if any, to encourage the development of these sources?

THE SOLAR HOUSE

Many builders now look for ways to use solar energy in the houses they build. You can do a series of projects from which you can learn basic principles of construction of a solar house.

Top: Natural volcanic steam "mined" at the Geysers in northern California can be used to generate electricity virtually pollution-free.
Bottom: This field of solar panels also generates electricity. Like geothermal steam, sunlight is free, and like geothermal energy, solar energy is clean.

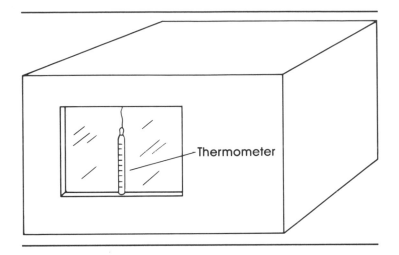

You can easily build a model of a solar home.

The simplest model house can consist of a wooden box with a single opening on one side. Cover the opening with a pane of glass, as shown in the figure. Hang a thermometer from the ceiling of the house. Now use this model to investigate ways in which solar energy can be used in the house.

You can test many factors with this model. First, remember that the sun is in different parts of the sky at different times of the day and different times of the year. You probably cannot rotate the house to keep up with the sun. So what is the best way to place the house on a lot in order to take advantage of sunlight throughout the year? Keep in mind that heat from the sun is usually an advantage during the winter months, but a disadvantage during the summer months.

Does it make any difference what the land topography is around the house? For example, suppose the house is built on flat land, on top of a hill, or into the side of a

Many homes now use solar panels to collect
sunlight for heat and hot water.

hill. Does the amount of solar energy captured by the house differ in these cases?

What effects do building materials have on the house's ability to capture and store solar energy? How efficient are bare wood, painted wood, brick, stucco, and other materials as building materials for the walls? Does the color of the walls make any difference? Does the interior floor material or the roofing material have any effect on the amount of heat captured by the house?

During the day, solar energy absorbed by the house will raise its interior temperature. But at night, the house will cool down. How can you save the heat captured during the day to use at night or to use for other purposes?

You will be able to think of many changes in your model house to test these and other factors. The more your model looks like a real house, the better your answers will be. But you can't build a real house. So try to make your model as realistic as possible while keeping it simple enough to work with.

You could also test the effectiveness of solar cells placed on the roof of the house. How much electrical energy can you generate with just one cell? With an array of six cells? With larger arrays? How could this electrical energy be used in the house? What are the advantages and disadvantages of using solar cells to generate electricity in houses being built in your community today? Prepare a report that lists your suggestions about the potential for solar houses in your community.

When you have completed these projects, talk with an architect or a representative of a solar energy company. Discuss your results and report with this person. Ask for an assessment of your findings. See page 95 for a photograph of a "real" solar house.

Finally, consider any applications to commercial buildings that your findings may have. Did you discover specific ideas that could and should be adopted in office buildings, shops, factories, and other nonresidential buildings?

7

ENVIRONMENTAL POLLUTION

The 1990s have seen a renewed interest in our environment. People around the world are becoming more concerned about the damage that humans are doing to our air, water, soil, and other natural resources. In most cases, environmental damage occurs as a result of some improvement in our life-style. For example, using private automobiles for transportation is a great convenience. But the more cars we use, the more contamination we add to the air.

Thus, the question of environmental pollution often becomes one of choices. Is a certain activity (such as driving private automobiles) of sufficient value to accept the environmental damage (such as air pollution) that activity may cause? Or is protection of the environment important enough to demand some cutback on the activity? The projects in this chapter give you an opportunity to explore some current environmental issues and the kinds of choices people have to make with respect to these issues.

On a clear day in Los Angeles, you can see
the snowcapped mountains to the north almost
all the way from the ocean! On a more typical
day, smog prevents you from even seeing
the nearby office buildings.

AIR POLLUTION

Analyzing air for pollutants is a relatively difficult task. If you would like to do a project on this topic, consult a high school or college chemistry teacher. That person may show you how to use specially designed kits used in testing for air pollutants. Some suppliers of these kits are listed in the appendix. You could also interview a representative from your local environmental control agency. That person may be willing to let you assist him or her in conducting tests for the agency.

One issue you can investigate is the effect of certain air pollutants on living organisms. You may know that carbon dioxide, sulfur dioxide, nitrogen oxides, and other air pollutants are known to damage plants and animals (including humans). These pollutants are risky to work with, so use only those mentioned below and work only under the careful supervision of an adult partner.

Set up a test plot in a 10-gallon aquarium. Cover the bottom of the aquarium with about 15 cm of soil. Plant about a dozen marigold plants in the soil. Cover the aquarium with a glass plate that fits tightly. Place the aquarium in a location where it will receive good sunlight (for the plants' sake) and good ventilation (for your sake). You can test the effect of various pollutants on plant growth using this test plot.

Set up a control plot in exactly the same way. The test plot and control plot are identical in every respect except for the experimental factors you introduce into the former. The control plot allows you to see how the marigold plants will grow normally, without the presence of any pollutants.

Studying Sulfur Dioxide

Safety Notes

1.   Wear safety goggles and a lab coat or lab apron while working on this project.

2. Sulfur dioxide is toxic and has a very strong, offensive, irritating odor. Do not breathe sulfur dioxide fumes.

3. Hydrochloric acid is toxic, and its fumes are very irritating. It can damage skin and clothing. If you spill any on yourself, wash it off with water.

4. Sodium sulfite is toxic. If you spill any on yourself, wash the area immediately with water.

Do this experiment only in a fume hood. Avoid breathing any fumes. Work only under the supervision of a qualified science teacher.

Ask your science teacher to introduce sulfur dioxide gas into the test plot for you. One way to do this is to place a 50-mL beaker in one corner of the aquarium, put 1 g of sodium sulfite into the beaker, add 10 mL of dilute (6N) hydrochloric acid to the beaker, and cover the aquarium *immediately.* Make sure the plants get enough natural or artificial sunlight. Observe the effect of sulfur dioxide on the plants for a period of about one week. Make a note of any changes you see.

The concentration of sulfur dioxide in this example is much greater than it is even in very polluted air. What effects would smaller concentrations of sulfur dioxide have on the plants? Do you see the same results occurring more slowly, or can you detect different kinds of changes?

What is the effect of exposing plants to sulfur dioxide for longer periods of time? In the real world, plants sometimes have to grow up and live all their lives in polluted air. Devise a project that will show how such plants may be different from those that grow in clean air.

Do other plants respond the same way to sulfur dioxide as did the marigolds? Try planting other flowers, fruits, and vegetables in your test plot to find out. Be aware that you may need to clean out your test plot between projects. Does sulfur dioxide enter the soil during one of these projects? Recall that a test for sulfur dioxide is given on page 29 of this book. If the soil in the aquarium becomes contaminated with sulfur dioxide, you will need to replace it with clean soil.

Studying Nitrogen Oxides

Safety Notes

1.   Wear safety goggles, gloves, and a lab apron or lab coat during this project.

2.   Some nitrogen oxides have an irritating odor. Do not smell any of the nitrogen oxides produced in the reaction.

3.   Hydrochloric acid is toxic, and its fumes are irritating. It can damage skin and clothing. If you spill any on yourself, wash it off with water.

4.   Potassium nitrite is toxic. If you spill any on yourself, wash immediately with water.

Do this experiment only in a fume hood. Avoid breathing any fumes. Be sure to work under the supervision of a qualified science teacher.

A second component of polluted air consists of oxides of nitrogen. Nitrogen forms five different oxides, all of which may be present to some extent in polluted air. You can generate three of these oxides by adding 1 mL of dilute (6N) hydrochloric acid to 1 g of potassium nitrite in a 50-mL beaker, as you did for the sulfur dioxide project. Since you will be working in a fume hood, make sure the plants get enough natural or artificial sunlight. Observe any changes in your test plants for one week.

Again, the concentration of nitrogen oxides produced according to these directions is much greater than that in actual polluted air. Try varying the concentration of nitrogen oxides and the types of plants used to determine how these factors affect your results.

Studying Particulates

A third component of polluted air is particulates. Particulates are tiny pieces of solid matter that are suspended in air. Soot—tiny particles of unburned carbon—is one form of particulate.

One way of testing the effect of particulates on plant growth is by adding chalk dust to your test plot. Clap two chalkboard erasers together in the air above your test plants. Replace the top on the aquarium and observe the plants for a week. How can you measure the amount of dust added to the aquarium in this way? Can you think of a more precise way to add particulates to your test plot? What is the effect of varying the amount of particulates added?

Recognizing the damage done by air pollutants in your community can be difficult. Sometimes it takes a long time for those effects to show up. You may need to ask an expert to show you examples of plants, buildings, and other objects that have been damaged by pollutants.

Interview a representative of the local environmental protection agency. Find out where air pollution has had an effect on crops, timber, animals, buildings, sculptures, and other objects in your community. Can this damage be traced to specific causes, such as a crowded expressway, a steel mill, a power-generating plant, or some other source? What specific attempts are being made to reduce the damage from air pollution in the community?

ACID RAIN

A special type of air pollution about which you may have heard is acid rain. The term "acid rain" refers to natural rainfall that is more acidic than normal. Many aspects of acid rain are the subject of considerable debate. For example, most scientists think that acid rain has at least some harmful effects on plants, animals, soil, and water. Other scientists are not so sure.

The acidity of rain is measured on the pH scale. The pH of any water solution ranges from about 0 to about 14. Acidic solutions have a pH of less than 7. Solutions with a pH greater than 7 are said to be basic. Pure water has a pH of exactly 7.

Natural rainfall has a pH of about 6. The most acidic rainfall ever measured had a pH of 2.4, about equal to the pH of lemon juice.

The pH of a solution is most easily measured with a device called a pH meter. Ask a chemistry teacher to demonstrate the use of a pH meter. You can also measure pH with indicator paper. Indicator paper changes color depending on the pH of the solution being tested. Your adult partner can demonstrate the use of indicator paper in determining the pH of a solution.

Determine the pH of rain that falls on your community. Collect a few milliliters of rain in a clean, dry beaker. Use either a pH meter or indicator paper to measure the pH of this rainwater. Repeat this project during three successive rain storms. Find out whether the pH of your rain changes over time. Note: You can also measure the pH of snow, fog, or any other form of precipitation. What changes do you have to make for forms of precipitation other than rain?

What human factors affect the pH of rain in your community? You can find out more about acid rain and factors that may cause it in various reference books. Ask your librarian for some suggestions. Or interview someone from the community's environmental protection agency, a representative of the local Sierra Club, or someone from another group interested in environmental issues in your community.

Devise a project or series of projects to discover the effects of acid rains on plants, animals, and nonliving materials. You can use a solution of commercial vinegar for these projects. Determine the pH of the vinegar with a pH meter or indicator paper. Then try diluting the vinegar with an equal volume of distilled water, with twice the volume of distilled water, with three times the volume of distilled water, and so on. Find the pH of each diluted solution.

With the original and diluted solution of vinegar, you can study the effects of acid rain on the materials you test.

Here are some ideas for possible projects:

1. Study the effects on lakes into which acid rain has fallen. Make a model lake by filling a 250-mL beaker half full with distilled water. Then add 5 mL of your acid rain solution to the aquarium. Drop a 3-cm square of cotton cloth into the model lake and see what happens to the cloth over a one-week period of time.

Repeat the experiment using other materials such as various types of cloth, various types of stone, various types of metal, and leaves and flowers from various plants.

2. Ask a biology teacher for a colony of some organism to test in your model lake. Daphnia are one good choice. Observe the behavior of the organisms in the model lake over a period of time. See how various concentrations of acid rain in the lake affect the organisms.

3. Add a small piece of limestone to your model lake. The limestone represents one type of rock that makes up the bottom of some lakes. Repeat one or more of the projects from 1 and 2 above. How are the results different when the model lake has a limestone bottom?

Lake bottoms are also made of sandstone, granite, and other types of rock. Add a piece of some other type of rock to your model lake to see how other lake bottoms influence the way acid rain affects materials and organisms.

4. Study the effects of acid rain on various materials. Suspend one or more of the materials listed in 1 above with a clothespin from a wire. Spray each material with a fine mist of acid rain solution. Observe the effect of a light spray once a day; a light spray three times a day; a heavy spray once a day; a heavy spray three times a day. How do different concentrations of acid rain in spray form affect the materials?

5. Spray acid rain solutions of various concentrations on various types of living plants. How does any one kind of plant respond to solutions of various concentrations? How does any one concentration of acid rain affect different kinds of plants?

Based on your research and your readings, what regions of the United States, Canada, and the rest of the world are likely to experience acid rain problems? Select any one of these regions to study in more detail. Ask your librarian for help in finding useful resources. Prepare a report that explains why acid rain is a problem in that area, how the problem might be solved, and what social factors might make it difficult to achieve this solution.

OBSERVING WATER POLLUTION

Contamination of a local pond, stream, lake, harbor, bay, bayou, or other body of water is a problem in almost every community in the United States. Choose a body of water in your community to study for water pollution.

In many cases, evidence of contaminated water is easy to find (see photograph). Old tires lying along the edge of the water, an oil slick floating on the water, mounds of scum on the water's surface, and plastic bottles and tin cans bobbing everywhere are typical indications of polluted waters.

To begin this project, walk along the body of water you have chosen to study. Make a list of obvious, visible evidence like the items mentioned above. For each item you list, speculate where that item may have come from, how it got into the water, and what risk it might pose for the community.

You can learn a great deal more about the water quality simply by making careful observations of the area. The U.S. Soil Conservation Service has developed a set of field sheets that can be used to check for the presence

of sediment, animal wastes, nutrients, pesticides, and salinity in water. These sheets allow you to give a numerical score to a body of water. The score indicates how polluted that water is. Table 6 is a slightly revised field sheet for animal wastes. Use this sheet to obtain a numerical score for the presence of animal wastes in the body of water you have chosen to study.

To rate water quality in relation to contamination by animal waste, refer to Table 6. If you rate water quality as described below, please do not write in this book. Instead, photocopy Table 6. At the top of the copy (or on the back), type or write in the following information: name of evaluator, county/state, water body evaluated, water body location, and the date evaluated. (If you don't have access to a copying machine, prepare a field sheet with the above information before proceeding.)

Then circle the appropriate numbers on the field sheet (or note the numbers on your homemade field sheet). Choose one number among the four choices in each row which best describes the conditions of the watercourse or water body being evaluated. If a condition has characteristics of two categories, you can "split" the score.

Now add the Rating Item scores to get a total for the field sheet. Write down the ranking for this site based on the total field score. Write "Excellent" for a score of 35–43, "Good" for 21–34, "Fair" for 7–20, and "Poor" for 6 or less. Record your total score and rank (excellent, good, etc.) on the copy of the field sheet or on your homemade version.

Is there a stream like this near you? Or is it a pond, an open sewer, or a dump? Call it what you will, it makes an excellent subject for an STS project.

TABLE 6

Animal Waste

Evaluator _____

Water Body Evaluated _____   Water Body Location _____   County/State _____   Date _____

Total Score/Rank _____

Rating Item	Excellent	Good	Fair	Poor
1. Evidence of animal waste: visual and olfactory	:-- No manure in or near water body. :-- No odor. :-- OTHER 9	:-- Occasional manure droppings where cattle cross or are in water. :-- Slight musk odor. :-- OTHER 6	:-- Manure droppings in concentrated localized areas. :-- Strong manure or ammonia odor. :-- OTHER 2	:-- Dry and wet manure all over banks or in water. :-- Strong manure & ammonia odor. :-- OTHER 0
2. Turbidity & color (observe in slow water)	:-- Clear or slightly greenish water in pond or along the whole reach of stream. :-- No noticeable colored film on submerged objects or rocks. :-- OTHER 9	:-- Occasionally turbid or cloudy. Water stirred up & muddy & brownish at animal crossings. :-- Pond water greenish. :-- Rocks or submerged objects covered with thin coating of green, olive, or brown build-up less than 5 mm thick. :-- OTHER 6	:-- Stream & pond water bubbly, brownish and cloudy where muddied by animal use. :-- Pea green color in ponds when not stirred up by animals. :-- Bottom covered w/green or olive film. Rocks or submerged objects coated with heavy or filamentous build-up 5-75 mm thick or long. :-- OTHER 3	:-- Stream & pond water brown to black, occasionally with a manure crust along banks. :-- Sluggish & standing water—murky and bubbly (foaming). :-- Ponds often bright green or with brown/black decaying algal mats. :-- OTHER 0

3. Amount of aquatic vegetation	-- Little vegetation—uncluttered look to stream or pond. -- What you would expect for a pristine water body in area. -- Usually fairly low amounts of many different kinds of plants. -- OTHER 8	-- Moderate amounts of vegetation; *or* -- What you would expect for the naturally occurring site-specific conditions. -- OTHER 6	-- Cluttered weedy conditions. -- Vegetation sometimes luxurious and green. -- Seasonal algal blooms. -- OTHER 3	-- Choked weedy conditions or heavy algal blooms or no vegetation at all. -- Dense masses of slimy white, greyish green, rusty brown or black water molds common on bottom. -- OTHER 0
4. Fish behavior in hot weather; fish kills, especially before dawn	-- No fish piping or aberrant behavior. -- No fish kills. -- OTHER 8	-- In hot climates, occasional fish piping or gulping for air in ponds just before dawn. -- No fish kills in last two years. -- OTHER 5	-- Fish piping common just before dawn. -- Occasional fish kills. -- OTHER 3	-- Pronounced fish piping. -- Pond fish kills common. -- Frequent stream fish kills during spring thaw. -- Very tolerant species (e.g., bullhead, catfish). -- OTHER 0
5. Bottom dwelling aquatic organisms	-- Intolerant species occur: mayflies, stoneflies, caddisflies, water penny, riffle beetle and a mix of tolerants. -- High diversity. -- OTHER 9	-- A mix of tolerants: shrimp, damselflies, dragonflies, black flies. -- Intolerants rare. -- Moderate diversity. -- OTHER 5	-- Many tolerants (snails, shrimp, damselflies, dragonflies, black flies). -- Mainly tolerants and some very tolerants. -- Intolerants rare. -- Reduced diversity with occasional upsurges of tolerants, e.g. tube worms, and chironomids. -- OTHER 3	-- Only tolerants or very tolerants: midges, craneflies, horseflies, rat-tailed maggots, or none at all. -- Very reduced diversity. upsurges of very tolerants common. -- OTHER 0

You can get further information about this field sheet, about other field sheets, and about this kind of water testing from local offices of the Soil Conservation Service or the Department of Agriculture. Ask for publication SCS-TP-161, "Water Quality Indicators Guide: Surface Water."

This publication also explains how the land area adjacent to a body of water can be studied. For example, animal wastes contaminating a pond must have come from somewhere. As you study your body of water, observe the land near it. What possible sources of water pollution (animals, bags of fertilizers, pesticide spraying machines, a field of abandoned cars, etc.) do you find? What connections can you make between the land and water that you study?

TESTING FOR WATER POLLUTANTS
AND THEIR EFFECTS

You can perform chemical tests on water to measure its degree of pollution. Some companies that sell water testing kits are listed in the appendix. A local high school or college may have such kits for you to borrow and work with. Ask an adult partner to show you how to use such kits. Then do a chemical analysis of the body of water you have chosen to study.

Some chemical tests are easy and safe to perform. You should ask your adult partner to work with you on these. For example, you can determine the acidity of water with a pH meter or indicator paper. Collect a sample of water from about five different locations along the stream or lake you are studying. Place the samples in stoppered, labeled bottles, and test them as soon as possible after collection. Record the pH of each sample you test. Decide whether the acidity of your water samples changes in any regular way (for example, from upstream to downstream on a river).

How do various water pollutants affect organisms that live in the water? You can try answering that question with a model lake. Fill a 500-mL beaker about two-thirds full with tap water. Now choose an organism to add to the model lake. Daphnia are a good test animal. A biology teacher may suggest other organisms to test and may give you some of these organisms.

Add 1 mL of motor oil to your model lake, and for 24 hours observe any changes in the organisms you are studying. Repeat your observations once a day every day for a week. Keep a record of any changes you see in the organisms.

How does changing the amount of motor oil added to the model lake affect your results? Are other organisms more or less sensitive to the effects of oil in water? Devise other projects that will provide answers to these questions. Consult with a biology teacher about organisms that are and are not appropriate to use in these projects.

What is the effect of other contaminants on water plants and animals? For example, at what pH does water begin to have harmful effects on daphnia? On other organisms? Plan a project that will measure the effect of acidity on various organisms.

Another contaminant in some bodies of water is heat. Power-generating plants and factories sometimes use lake or river water for cooling purposes. After use, the water is returned to the lake or river usually at a warmer temperature than when it was taken out. What is the effect on water plants and animals of exposure to this heated water?

Purchase some elodea plants at the local pet shop. See how increasing the temperature in your model lake by 1°, 2°, 5°, etc. affects the way these plants grow. You will need to think, first of all, of a safe, dependable way of increasing the water temperature in your model lake. How do similar changes in temperature affect animals that live in the water?

Talk with your adult partner about water pollution problems in your community. Your local environmental protection agency or water department is a good place to look for an expert on this topic. Make a map of your community that shows polluted bodies of water. Indicate on the map the kinds of pollution found in each place and the possible sources of such pollution. Why does the pollution in each case continue to exist? What factors—scientific, technological, political, economic—have prevented the pollution problem from being resolved? Come up with some new approaches for reducing water pollution in your community. Ask your adult partner or an expert on water pollution to evaluate your suggestions.

8

POPULATION

The cause of most of today's world problems is population growth. The more people a nation has, the more natural resources it uses up, and the more waste and pollution it produces. Growing populations also increase the demand for food and medical services. The world cannot hope to solve its most serious problems until it brings population growth under control.

At least that is what many of the world's population experts believe.

But some authorities hold quite a different view. The official position of the United States government, for example, is that population growth is not the cause of starvation, hunger, disease, shortages, and pollution. Instead, the U.S. government and some population experts argue that population growth is good. According to this view, the more people a country has, the better its chances of solving its problems.

No one is sure which of these opinions is a better explanation of the world's population problems. What nearly everyone does agree on is that anyone interested in issues of science, technology, and society today must understand some basic ideas about population growth. The projects in this chapter will help you develop that understanding.

POPULATION GROWTH

Probably the most basic information you need to know is how population growth has changed over time. Begin by making two graphs, one of the estimated world population and one of the population of the United States, both over the last three centuries. You can find this information in encyclopedias, almanacs, the *Statistical Abstract of the United States,* and books on population.

What overall trends do you find in changes in the world and U.S. populations between 1700 (or earlier) and today? What factors do you think may account for these trends? What is the significance of these trends for today's world and that of the future?

Try to find someone in the community who knows about population issues. A representative of Planned Parenthood or a local college or high school teacher might be such a person. Present your graphs and your interpretations of them to this adult partner. What views on these trends does she or he have?

Construct a population graph for your own community. Your city or town clerk, the local historical society, the librarian, or a high school or college teacher will help you find the data you need. How can you explain the trends you see in your own community's population graph?

Does your community have a "population problem"? If so, what is the nature of that problem? Talk with someone from the local planning board or anyone else interested in your town's population. Write a brief newspaper article that explains why the citizens of your community should know more about its population growth, past, present, and future.

A CEMETERY SURVEY

In most parts of the world, people are living longer now than they ever have. This fact is very important in understanding population issues today. Can you think why it is so important? Is that pattern also true for your community?

You can find out more about the way life expectancies in your community have changed over the years by doing a cemetery survey. To do this project, visit one or more cemeteries in your community. Choose about a hundred tombstones at random to study. Make sure you include some of the oldest tombstones, some of the newest, and some from all periods in between. You want to get tombstone data from every period of your community's history.

From each of the tombstones you visit, write down the age of the person at her or his death. Then make a graph that shows the average age to which a person lived for each 20-year period in your community's history. For example, you might find that between 1910 and 1930, the average age at death from ten tombstones studied was 54 years. Then you might find that between 1930 and 1950, the average age at death from 12 tombstones was 63 years. These two pieces of data give you two points on your graph. (You may need to change the 20-year period to some other length of time, depending on how old your community is.)

Based on your cemetery survey, what can you say about how life expectancies have changed over the years in your community? What new problems has your community had to face because of these changes in life expectancy?

You can collect similar information by examining obituary columns in your local newspaper. How can you modify the cemetery survey project using obituaries instead of tombstones? Which method is likely to give you more reliable results?

CHANGING DEATH RATES

Many factors account for falling death rates. One of the most important is the conquest of disease. Medical science has learned how to prevent and cure many illnesses that once killed millions of people. The purpose of this project is to find out how the death rate from various causes has changed over time in various locations. You should try to discover how death rates from pneumonia, yellow fever, cancer, and other causes has changed from 1700 to the present day in your community, in the United States, and in other nations.

Information on causes of death is available from many sources. In your own community, the health department will probably have records that go back many years. A representative of that department can give you this information or tell you where else to look for it. County and state health departments have similar records for those levels of government.

National records on causes of death can be found in the *Statistical Abstract,* in almanacs, and in encyclopedias.

The World Health Organization keeps health records for most nations of the world. You may also be able to get such records from health agencies in individual nations. Write the U.S. embassy of the nation or nations that you want to study.

Use these sources to identify patterns in causes of death in (1) your own community, (2) your state, (3) the United States, and (4) one country from List A and one from List B below. Find an interesting and informative way to summarize your findings.

List A	List B
Canada	Brazil
France	Egypt
Great Britain	Ethiopia
Israel	India
Japan	Indonesia

Sweden	Mexico
Switzerland	Nigeria

Compare changing death rates in the localities you studied. Especially important are the comparisons of death rates in the United States, countries in List A, and countries in List B. How do you account for the differences you find? What significance do these differences have for each country today?

GUESSES ABOUT THE FUTURE

One aim of population studies is to make projections about future trends. Members of your local school board, for example, need to know how the population of your community will change over the next 20 years. Why? What other governmental agencies are likely to be interested in population projections? Why are estimates of future population changes of interest to private companies?

The graph on page 118 shows population trends in a fictitious town over the past 100 years. The dotted lines show three projections for the future. Line A shows population changes over the next 20 years if past trends continue into the future. Line B shows what will happen if the rate of population growth increases. And line C shows what will happen if the community's rate of growth falls off.

For this project, try to decide which of these three population projections is most likely to be correct for your own community. You might decide that some other projection is better than any of these three. Try to find government reports, articles, or other information on the following factors for your community.

1. Birthrate.

2. Death rate.

3. Rate of immigration.

4. Rate of emigration.

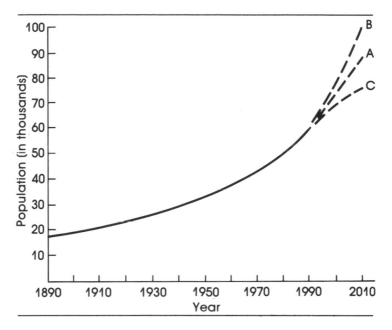

A graph of population change in a fictitious town over the past one hundred years.

Based on this information, choose any one of the three dotted lines in the figure—or draw one of your own—that estimates population changes in your community over the next 20 years.

What does this projection mean for various elements in your community? For example, how should the public school system, community hospital(s), the parks and recreation department, local industries, and other community groups make use of this projection?

Choose any one government agency or one local business for whom to answer this question. Prepare a 20-year plan, a list of recommendations for action for this agency or company in the future. Then, talk with a representative of that agency or company. Many organizations make projections like those you did for this project. How did the projections of the organization you chose compare to the ones you made? Find out how the agency representative you talk to agrees and disagrees with your analysis, projections, and recommendations.

POPULATION KNOWLEDGE AND ATTITUDES

What do people in your community know about population issues? What attitudes do they have about such issues? Write a questionnaire that will allow you to answer this question for a selection of your friends and neighbors.

What information about population should people in your community have? Make a list of "essential facts" you think people should know. Among those facts might be answers to the following:

1. What is the population of [your community]?

2. How has the community's population changed in the last 20 years?

3. What is the population of the United States? How has it changed in the last 20 years?

4. What three nations in the world have the fastest-growing population? Which three have the slowest-growing population?

5. What is the official government policy on population growth in the United States? In the rest of the world?

6. What is the most important single factor affecting population growth in the world today?

Of course, you will want to be sure you know the answers to these and other questions you ask people.

Prepare a list of "opinion" questions, too. Find out how people in your community feel about various population issues. Some of the questions you might ask include the following:

1.   Do you favor an increase, decrease, or stabilization in [your community's] population? Why?

2.   What should the community government do to bring about the change you favor in question 1?

3.   Is world population growth an issue of concern to you? Why or why not? Is population growth in the United States of concern? Why or why not?

4.   Do you believe that population growth is related to other social, political, and economic problems? If so, give one example. If not, why not?

5.   Do you think students in high school should study population issues? Why or why not?

Again, it will be helpful if you have some idea about current viewpoints on such issues. Consult the *Reader's Guide to Periodical Literature,* books on population, and your librarian for assistance.

Your final report should describe how informed the people in your community are about population issues. It should also summarize their viewpoints on various population questions. In your report, explain what needs to be done to educate people in the community about population and what issues may need to be addressed by local government and private agencies.

APPENDIX

Suppliers of Kits and Equipment

Carolina Biological Supply
2700 York Road
Burlington, NC 27215
(919) 584-0381

Central Scientific Company
11222 Melrose Avenue
Franklin Park, IL 60131
(312) 451-0150

Connecticut Valley Biological
Supply
82 Valley Road, P.O. Box 326
Southampton, MA 01073
(800) 628-7748
(800) 282-7757 (MA only)

Fisher Scientific Company
4901 W. Le Moyne Street
Chicago, IL 60651
(800) 621-4769

Hach Company
P.O. Box 389
Loveland, CO 80539
(800) 525-5940

La Motte Chemical Products
Company
P.O. Box 329
Chestertown, MD 21620
(301) 778-3100 (MD)
(800) 344-3100 (elsewhere)

Forestry Suppliers, Inc.
205 W. Rankin St.
P.O. Box 8397
Jackson, MS 39284-8397
(800) 647-5368

Home Harvest Company; Hoyt
Hydroponic Garden Kit
9404 Genesee Avenue, #284
La Jolla, CA 92037
(619) 453-3081

Martinells Enterprises
P.O. Box 10369
Costa Mesa, CA 92627
(714) 645-1700

Nasco
901 Janesville Ave.
P.O. Box 901
Fort Atkinson, WI 53538-0901
(800) 558-9595

FOR FURTHER READING

CHAPTER ONE: SCIENCE, TECHNOLOGY, AND SOCIETY

Beller, Joel. *So You Want to Do a Science Project!* New York: Arco, 1982.

Challand, Helen. *Activities in the Earth Sciences.* Chicago: Childrens Press, 1982.

————. *Activities in the Life Sciences.* Chicago: Childrens Press, 1982.

————. *Science Projects and Activities.* Chicago: Childrens Press, 1983.

Council on Environmental Quality Staff. *Environmental Quality: Annual Report.* [n.p./n.d.] This report is supposed to be published annually.

————. *The Global Two Thousand Report to the President: Entering the Twenty-First Century,* Volume I. New York: Penguin, 1982.

Enger, Eldon D., J. Richard Kormelink, Bradley F. Smith, and Rodney J. Smith. *Environmental Science: The Study of Relationships.* Dubuque, Iowa: Wm. C. Brown, 1986.

Iritz, Maxine. *Science Fair: Developing a Successful and Fun Project.* Blue Ridge Summit, Pa.: TAB Books, 1987.

Kupchella, Charles E., and Margaret C. Hyland. *Environmental Science: Living within the System of Nature.* Boston: Allyn and Bacon, 1986.

Moran, Joseph M., Michael D. Morgan, and James H. Wiersma.

Introduction to Environmental Science, 2d ed. New York: W. H. Freeman, 1986.

Newton, David E. *Science and Social Issues.* Portland, Maine: J. Weston Walch, 1987.

ReVelle, Penelope, and Charles ReVelle. *The Environment: Issues and Choices for Society,* 3d ed. Boston: Jones and Bartlett, 1988.

Smith, Norman F. *How to Do Successful Science Projects.* Englewood Cliffs, N.J.: Julian Messner, 1990.

Tocci, Salvatore. *How to Do a Science Fair Project.* New York: Franklin Watts, 1986.

Turk, Jonathan, and Amos Turk. *Environmental Science,* 3d ed. Philadelphia: Saunders, 1984.

Van Deman, Barry A., and Ed McDonald. *Nuts and Bolts: A Matter of Fact Guide to Science Fair Projects.* Harwood Heights, Ill.: Science Man Press, 1980.

CHAPTER TWO: FOOD AND NUTRITION

Lee, Sally. *New Theories on Diet and Nutrition.* New York: Franklin Watts, 1990.

Ontario Science Center Staff. *Foodworks: Over One Hundred Science Activities and Fascinating Facts that Explore the Magic of Food.* Reading, Mass.: Addison-Wesley, 1987.

Peavy, Linda, and Ursula Smith. *Food, Nutrition, and You.* New York: Macmillan, 1982.

Physician Task Force on Hunger in America. *Hunger in America.* Middletown, Conn.: Wesleyan University Press, 1985.

Public Health Service, U.S. Department of Health and Human Services. *The Surgeon General's Report on Nutrition and Health.* Washington, D.C.: Government Printing Office, 1988.

Robbins, John. *Diet for a New America.* Walpole, N.H.: Stillpoint Publishing, 1987.

Tobias, Alice L., and Patricia J. Thompson. *Issues in Nutrition for the 1980s.* Monterey, Calif.: Wadsworth Health Sciences Division, 1980.

Ward, Brian. *Diet and Nutrition.* New York: Franklin Watts, 1987.

CHAPTER THREE: AGRICULTURE

Fodor, R. V. *Chiseling the Earth: How Erosion Shapes the Land.* Hillside, N.J.: Enslow, 1983.

Gorman, Carol. *America's Farm Crisis.* New York: Franklin Watts, 1987.

National Gardening Association. *Grow Lab: A Complete Guide to Gardening in the Classroom.* Burlington, Vt.: National Gardening Association, 1988.

Rosenblum, John W., ed. *Agriculture in the Twenty-First Century.* New York: Wiley, 1983.

Soil and Water Conservation. Irving, Tex.: Boy Scouts of America, 1968.

CHAPTER FOUR: LAND AND WATER USE

Biological Sciences Curriculum Study (BSCS). *Investigating the Human Environment: Land Use.* Dubuque, Iowa: Kendall/Hunt, 1984.

Burchell, Robert W., and Edward E. Duensing, eds. *Land Use Issues for the 1980s.* Piscataway, N.J.: Center for Urban Policy Research, 1982.

Goldin, Augusta. *Water: Too Much, Too Little, Too Polluted.* San Diego: Harcourt Brace Jovanovich, 1983.

Newton, David E. *Land Use: A to Z.* Hillside, N.J.: Enslow, 1991.

Porter, Paul R., and David C. Sweet. *Rebuilding America's Cities: Roads to Recovery.* New Brunswick, N.J.: Center for Urban Policy Research, 1984.

Pringle, Laurence. *Water: The Next Great Resource Battle.* New York: Macmillan, 1982.

CHAPTER FIVE: SOLID WASTES

American Chemical Society. *Cleaning Our Environment—A Chemical Perspective,* 2d ed. Washington, D.C.: American Chemical Society, 1978.

Hayes, Dennis. *Repairs, Reuse, Recycling—First Steps Toward a Sustainable Society.* Washington, D.C.: Worldwatch Institute, 1978.

Melosi, M. V. *Garbage in the Cities.* College Station, Tex.: Texas A&M University Press, 1982.

Miller, Christina G., and Louise A. Berry. *Wastes.* New York: Franklin Watts, 1986.

Pringle, Laurence. *Throwing Things Away: From Middens to Resource Recovery.* New York: Harper and Row, 1986.

CHAPTER SIX: ENERGY

BSCS Study Staff. *Energy and Society: Investigations in Decision-Making.* Northbrook, Ill.: Hubbard Scientific, 1977.

Cook, James G. *Thomas Edison Book of Easy and Incredible Experiments.* New York: John Wiley and Sons, 1988.

Fogel, Barbara F. *Energy: Choices for the Future.* New York: Franklin Watts, 1985.

Gardner, Robert. *Energy Projects.* New York: Franklin Watts, 1987.

Gibson, Michael. *The Energy Crisis.* Vero Beach, Fla.: Rourke, 1987.

Gordon, Glen, and William Keifer. *The Delicate Balance: An En-*

ergy and the Environment Chemistry Module. New York: Harper and Row, 1980.

Grolier Editors, and John H. Douglas. *The Future World of Energy.* New York: Franklin Watts, 1984.

Siegel, Mark A., et al. *Energy: An Issue of the Eighties.* Wylie, Tex.: Information Plus, 1989.

CHAPTER SEVEN: ENVIRONMENTAL POLLUTION

Berger, Melvin. *Hazardous Substances: A Reference.* Hillside, N.J.: Enslow, 1986.

The Conservation Foundation. *State of the Environment: An Assessment at Mid-Decade.* Washington, D.C.: The Conservation Foundation, 1984.

Hessler, Edward W., and Harriet Stubbs. *Acid Rain Science Projects.* St. Paul, Minn.: Acid Rain Foundation, 1987.

Miller, Christina G., and Louise A. Berry. *Acid Rain.* Englewood Cliffs, N.J.: Messner, 1987.

Newton, David E. *Taking a Stand Against Environmental Pollution.* New York: Franklin Watts, 1990.

Pawlick, Thomas. *A Killing Rain: The Global Threat of Acid Precipitation.* San Francisco: Sierra Club Books, 1984.

Pringle, Laurance. *Lives at Stake: The Science and Politics of Environmental Health.* New York: Macmillan, 1980.

Thackray, Sue. *Looking at Pollution.* North Pomfret, Vt.: David and Charles, 1987.

CHAPTER EIGHT: POPULATION

Ehrlich, Paul R. *Population Bomb,* new, rev. ed. New York: Ballantine, 1986.

Jacobson, Willard J. *Population Education: A Knowledge Base.* New York: Teacher's College, Columbia University, 1979.

McGraw, Eric. *Population Growth.* Vero Beach, Fla.: Rourke, 1987.

Nam, Charles B. *Think about Our Populations: The Changing Face of America.* New York: Walker, 1988.

Simon, Julian. *The Ultimate Resource.* Princeton, N.J.: Princeton University Press, 1982.

Wattenberg, Ben. *The Birth Dearth,* rev. ed. New York: Pharos Books, 1989.

Additional ideas for population projects can be obtained from the Population Reference Bureau, Inc., 777 14th Street, N.W., Suite 800, Washington, DC 20005; (202) 639-8040.

INDEX

Page numbers in *italics* indicate illustrations.

Drought, *59*
Dump, *68*, 73–76, *75;* unofficial, 74–76
Dust storm, 56

Elodea plants, 111
Energy, 79–96; alternative sources of, 91–93; problems related to use of, 79
Energy conservation, 84–86
Energy cost distribution, 81
Energy use: in business and industry, 83–84; and private automobile, 86–88
Environmental effects, of energy use, 79
Environmental pollution, 97–112
Erosion, *51, 56;* and human activities, 53–55; and rainfall, 52; topography and, 52. *See also* Land erosion; Natural erosion; Wind erosion
Evaporation, 41

Farmland, building on, *54*
Farmland runoff, environmental problems from, 42–43
Fast foods, 22–24
Fertilizers, effects of, 37–39
Field sheets, 105–110
Food, and nutrition, 21–32
Food additives, 24–26; risks and benefits of, 27–28; testing for, 28–30
Food preservation, methods of, 24–26

Geothermal power, 91
Goals, of STS projects, 12–13
Greenpeace, 13

Heat, as contaminant, 111
Herbicides, 42

Home, waste problems of, 70–71
Home energy audit, 80–82

Indicator paper, 103, 110
Irrigation, 39–42, *40;* defined, 39
Irrigation ditch, 41

Kilowatt-hours (kwh), 80

Land: characteristics of, 57; legal restrictions on, 57; potential uses for, 57
Land erosion, testing for, 50
Land use, 55–57; in your community, 57–58
League of Women Voters, 87

Manure, 37, 39. *See also* Natural fertilizer
"Marine Debris and the Environment," *18*
Mathematical analysis, 12
Metric units, 20
Model lake, 111
Model plot: and land erosion, 50; studying agricultural methods with, 35–*36*

Natural erosion, 50–53
Natural fertilizers, 37. *See also* Manure
Nitrogen, test for, 44–45
Nitrogen oxides, studying, 101
Nutrition: foods and, 21–32; knowledge of, 31–32
"Nutritive Values of Foods," 22

Obituaries, 115

Packaged foods, 24
Particulates, studying, 101–102
Pesticides, 42